D0857374

Creativity and Disease

Copyright © 1982 by George F. Stickley Company
ISBN 0-89313-066-4
Library of Congress Catalog Number 82-50530
Fourth edition (Revised), 1987

Printed in Sweden by Bohusläningens Boktryckeri AB, Uddevalla 1986
Published by the George F. Stickley Company, 210 West Washington
Square, Phila., Pa. 19106.

Creativity and Disease

How illness affects literature, art and music

Philip Sandblom, M.D., Ph.D. h.c.

GEORGE F. STICKLEY COMPANY 210 W. WASHINGTON SQUARE
PHILADELPHIA, PA 19106

In great artists, the desire to create and the endeavour to immortalize a personal conception may overcome even extreme disability. Thus, despite painful old-age arthritis which obliged the artist to have cotton taped to the palm of his hand so as to be able to hold the brush between the thumb and the ring-finger, as we see in the self-portrait, Renoir painted pictures that radiate youthful joy, and took delight in representing children, young women and the flowers of spring.

For Grace

"*A Being breathing thoughtful breath,*
A Traveller between life and death;
The reason firm, the temperate will,
Endurance, foresight, strength, and skill;
A perfect Woman, nobly planned,
To warm, to comfort, and command;
And yet a Spirit still, and bright
With something of angelic light"[73]

Contents

Forewords

The treatise by my admired friend Philip Sandblom on "Creativity and Disease", for which I have been asked to write a short preface, testifies to the advantage of an inter-disciplinary approach to a humanistic theme that could not be adequately studied from one side only. The author carries the ideal prerequisites for such an approach by being at the same time an internationally renowned surgeon and a life-long lover of art for art's own sake.

Sandblom's double competence as a physician and an art connoisseur—both activities for which the eye is the supreme tool—asserts itself on every page of this book. It is indeed fascinating to follow under his guidance the mysterious links, sometimes for better, sometimes for worse, that exist between illness and creativity, in the past as well as in present time, in literature and music, as well as in art.

The richness of the theme, which in an almost kaleido-scopic fashion assumes ever new patterns, will, I am confident, appeal to both medical and humanistic readers. In fact, one of the merits of this book is that the author has been able to treat his subject both with serious under-standing and with something of the liveliness of an infor-mal talk. It is clearly by an author who has read much, seen much, heard much and thought much about the whole issue. Happily free from sentimentality, he invites us to share with him a deeper insight into many of art history's most poignant lifestories. Once you start read-ing, you will not easily put the book aside before having finished it.

Carl Nordenfalk, Ph.D.
Director emeritus of the Swedish National Museum

As gene splicing, molecular biology, automated clinical chemistry and CAT scanning gradually seem to be replacing artful physicians with glorified technicians, it is gratifying indeed to read a book by a cultured and sensitive physician whose concern is the interaction of soma and soul. Sandblom gives us a finely crafted historical survey of instances where illness affected creation.

To any cultured physician the psychopathology of expression is an intellectual challenge as much as it is a puzzle to creative artists themselves and to laymen who know and enjoy art. Works of art, written, visual or tonal, elicit in the beholder physical phenomena and psychic responses, akin to those that may have stirred their creators while producing the art.

Same day a smart young biochemist, who may or may not be a physician in the humanistic sense of the word, may clear up the mystery of how soma and psyche interact to produce or to react to works of art. He may find that this involves endorphins or other, as yet unnamed messengers within the body which interact with specific receptors after activation by complex hormonal and enzymatic mechanisms.

Such an investigator (if at his time people will still be able to read) may well have been inspired by Sandblom's overview of the interaction of illness and creation. Such is the hypothetical impact of this book on future medicine. For the present, it is certain that this articulate and erudite study by a cultured physician will give great pleasure and stimulation to all who appreciate and love art.

Freddy Homburger, M.D.
Research Professor of Pathology, Boston University School of Medicine

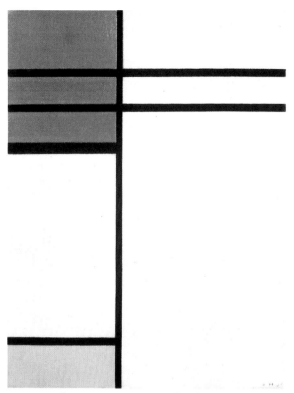

1. P. Mondrian, *Composition with red, 1936.*

Mondrian affirms his credo: "It is the line, the color and their relations which must bring into play the whole sensual and intellectual register of the inner life." Discussing this Composition with red, *1936, Butor[12] assures us that "Mondrian is clearly aware of the tragic character that a cross inside his composition can present", and he ventures to suggest that "this small red spot represents the fatal twilight with the sun setting tragically".*

Introduction

Per varios usus artem experientia fecit. (Manilius)
Through varied trials experience creates art.

"For most poets, poetry is but a current commentary on their private lives, a transcription into verse of the prose of their Fate." The author[55] who voiced this idea might well have extended it to the artist in general, because art is always founded on experience; one cannot create from nothing.

This truism must still seem meaningful since it is so often repeated and elaborated upon. Anton Chekhov, who had a medical education as well as his own tuberculosis to draw on, modestly admitted that "if I had only my imagination to rely on in attempting a career in literature, I should like to be excused". Henri Matisse [42] explains how "the artist works by incorporating and gradually assimilating the exterior world until the object which he designs has become as it were a part of himself—and he can project it on the canvas as his own creation". Gustav Mahler accepted the idea with these words: "creative art and actual experience are one and the same," but also indicated a modification, as one senses in his music: "a bit of mystery always remains, for the creator as well."

When considering different aspects of the conception to test its validity, one stumbles on abstract art—can that be founded on anything but sheer invention? Mondrian, one of the great protagonists, was eager to answer the question.[43] He says explicitly that "all that the non-figurative artist receives from the outside is not only

 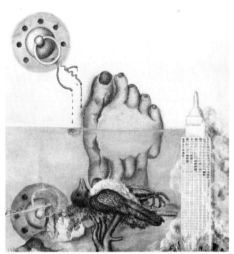

useful but indispensable, because it arouses in him the desire to create that which he only vaguely feels and which he could never represent in a true manner without the contact with visible reality and with the world which surrounds him" (Fig. 1).

The connection between art and experience is more convincing in realistic painting and may even be pathetically evident as in the case of Frida Kahlo, the Mexican surrealistic painter, wife of Diego Rivera. "I paint my own reality" she said, and a tearful, bleeding and painful reality it was. Her claim to a record number of operations was hardly an exaggeration since she underwent 32!

A famous American surgeon, Leo Eloesser, who became her doctor and her friend, found that she had an anomaly of the spine, *spina bifida*, causing progressive ulcerations of her legs and feet. As so often among patients with congenital defects, she preferred to blame her condition on some external cause. And well she might, since as a child she had polio, affecting her right leg, and later was badly injured in a traffic accident. Her spine, her pelvis and her foot were crushed, but not her

2. Frida Kahlo, The broken column, 1944. One of many self portraits of the artist suffering, her injured spine represented as a broken pillar.

3. Frida Kahlo, What the water gave me, 1938 (detail). The artist in the bathtub. Between her toes are the sores that are typical lesions attending the congenital defect of spina bifida. *"My foot continues to be sick—'trophic ulcer', what is that?" Even the broken stopper-chain bleeds in sympathy.*

forceful spirit. "I paint because I need to" she explained, depicting her suffering in a number of shockingly revealing self portraits. In one (Fig. 2) she is weeping from pain, represented as lacerating nails. The crushed spine on which she blames her misery is depicted as a broken column. But in another painting (Fig. 3), showing her lying in the bathtub, feet sticking out of the water, she gives herself away: the sores between the toes are typical lesions caused by her congenital defect, the *spina bifida*, probably the main cause of her suffering. In still another gruesome picture, she seems to be seeking our compassion when she pulls up her skirts to reveal a terrible gash on her thigh. Eventually her leg had to be amputated and she died soon after. In the words of her biographer[28] "she transmuted her pain into art with remarkable frankness, tempered by humor and fantasy".

Frida is an impressive example of the fact that severe illness exerts a critical influence on our lives, as well as on our creativity. One can accustom oneself to much–but not to pain, especially when it is lingering–as it then "is ever before us". Its bearing on the creative work of an artist would be particularly apparent to a physician, with his special knowledge of the nature of disease.

No two people view the surrounding world or a work of art with the same eyes, and our attention will be drawn to features of which we have special knowledge. I suppose, for example, that only a fellow physician can fully appreciate the horror of the poor, incompetent Doctor Bovary (in Flaubert's novel) who had been prevailed upon to try a new method of treating clubfoot (by enclosing the redressed limb in plaster) and shortly thereafter perceived a stench emanating through the bandage, a dismal foreboding of threatening gangrene. Thus to a large extent our perception of works of art, and for that matter of all that occurs around us, is influenced by our experience and education.

4. A. Strindberg,
Sea-marker in storm, 1892.
The author turned to
painting when he felt that
he had to give free outlet
to his tormented feelings.
At this time he was close to
insanity, wild, but not bewildered, as he still mas-
tered his demons, except
those of jealousy, and commented that "few people
are lucky enough to be
capable of madness". Later
he painted again when his
literary inspiration waned.

Relationship between illness and creativity

With a medical background and an interest in the arts, my attention was naturally drawn to the diseases of artists. Often I noticed a connection between their suffering and their art. My experience thus differs from that of some authors[25] who belittle the influence of illness on artistic creation, arguing that "it can only be a matter of speculation" and suggesting that everyday incidents and trivialities are equally or more important.

Rather, there are reasons to believe that connections between illness and art are close and common. When a number of tuberculous patients were encouraged to use painting as a means of occupational therapy,[37] it was found that the course of the illness was recorded with extraordinary accuracy in the individual's paintings: "The apprehension and despondency prior to haemoptysis or surgery, the sadness and apathy which follow such an event, the freshness and gaiety during convalescence – all are registered on the patient's pictures like entries in a diary."

A study of the relationship between the suffering and the works of artists who have been severely ill may enhance an insight into, and our understanding of their art. I cannot agree with those critics who proclaim that it is only the work itself which is worthy of serious interest and that the personal background of the creators is little more than anecdotal.

Among different kinds of art there is a close relationship in terms of form as well as content, and they often develop side by side; this is hardly surprising since they are closely linked with the general pattern of cultural evolution. But the development is not exactly parallel, and the formative arts tend at one time to be closer to literature, sometimes even to the political pamphlet, and at another time closer to music, with its abstract form. The occasionally striking similarities in expression between the different art forms sometimes enable one to illustrate and bring out the character of a particular work by comparing it with a corresponding example in another art form.

It throws some light on the difference in expressive quality of painting and writing to note that when the mentally restless Swedish author, August Strindberg, was upset and lacked the peace of mind necessary for literary work, he turned to painting, where he found it easier to express his tormented feelings (Fig. 4).

During many years of excursions through the provinces of art I have collected examples of artists, writers and composers in whose work I have found a convincing link between illness and creativity. With recourse only to the inert matter that survives an individual's sojourn on this earth, the medical diagnosis of a historical person is liable to remain obscure. To an experienced physician, however, the patient's history may well suffice to establish a diagnosis. In the present examples the evidence has on the whole been unequivocal. My list is not intended as a complete catalogue of human misery in art but rather a subjective rhapsody in black – disease is always an evil. Consequently, I do not claim to have scientific, statistical evidence. For that purpose, as a famous scientist suggested to me, I should have collected two control groups for comparison, one where ill artists had created seemingly healthy work, and another where healthy artists had created art of seemingly diseased origin. Failing that, I am well satisfied with the humanist's evidence, namely "the conviction of personal experience". The "two cultures" are still happily divorced.

A study of this kind would, I think, be of value even if one agreed with George Bernard Shaw, that "disease is not interesting; it is something do be done away with by general consent and that is all about it". John Updike adds that there are areas of life which cannot be made interesting to the reader: "Disease and pain, for instance, are of consuming concern to the person suffering from them, but their descriptions weary us within a few paragraphs." He comes close to proving his point with a lengthy account of his *psoriasis*,[64] but remains interesting and entertaining when he describes this "other presence co-occupying your body and singling you out from the happy herds of normal mankind", bringing humiliation and shame. His skin disease may even have preserved a great writer – Updike counted himself out of jobs that demand being presentable and was left "a worker in ink who can hide himself and send out a surrogate presence". Both authors changed their mind when they themselves became ill; Shaw developed a caustic interest in his own osteomyelitis (p. 95) and Updike wrote a delightful description of his appendicitis.[63]

Nietzsche found a greater interest in suffering when he observed that a malicious pleasure in the misfortune of others is a standard complement of human character. There is more kindness in Goethe's view that "our own pain teaches us to share the suffering of our fellow creatures"; it is through suffering and pain that we can identify with them: happiness may be incomprehensible, pain is easy to understand.

The meaning of human misery has rarely been treated more profoundly than in the *Book of Job*. Although "he was blameless and upright . . . and turned away from evil", Job was deprived of both family and wealth and afflicted with loathsome sores from the sole of his foot to the crown of his head—"The night racks my bones and the pain that gnaws me takes no rest." Cursing the day of his birth, Job desperately asked the old and eternal question, "Why must man suffer?"

Feeling that his question was unanswered and his fate unjust, he bursts out in defiance: "Oh, that I had one to hear me! I have had my say, let the Almighty answer me!"

In the original version of the tale Job remains a titanic blasphemer and does not yield; it is only in a later addition that he resigns: "I had heard of Thee by the hearing of the ear, but now my eye sees Thee; therefore I despise myself and repent in dust and ashes". He is supposed to understand that suffering is not a punishment but a humbling and a purification of the mind: "He delivers the afflicted by their affliction and opens their ear by adversity". In a happy and thus unlikely end Job is then rewarded for his surrender with the restoration of health and wealth—and even with a new family! As one of the first in a long tradition, Job found that suffering also affects the mood of expression: "My lyre is tuned to mourning, and my pipe to the voice of those who weep."

Ever since antiquity, artistic creation has been associated with physical stigma,[11] the conception of superior strength is inseparable from suffering. Philoctetes, the peerless archer of Greek mythology whose snakebite suppurated with a stench so horrible that his companions left him behind on a desert island, provides the essence in Sophocles' play: "I would have remained thoughtless and carefree as an animal if it had not been for the wounds . . . When the pain takes hold of me I know that I am human".[72] In Gide's version, Philoctetes adds that "I have learned to express myself better, now that I am no longer with men—and I took to telling the story of my sufferings, and if the phrase were very beautiful I was so much consoled; I even sometimes forgot my sadness by uttering it."

The idea that the artist derives his power from some mutilation he has suffered, that his wound sets him apart from other men, is widely accepted—only the English romantic school is an exception. Both Wordsworth and Coleridge thought that poetry depends upon a condition of positive health in the poet, a more than usual well-being. The German romantic school, on the other hand, found suffering interesting and valuable.[67] The idea is already intimated by Goethe in *Wilhelm Meisters Lehrjahre:* "About the beginning of my eighth year, I was seized with a bloodcough; and from that moment my soul became all feeling, all memory." Friedrich Schlegel relates his feelings about his near-fatal disease: "it had a fuller and deeper nature than the ordinary health of others, who seemed rather like dreaming sleepwalkers". Novalis, the poet of death, who died at 28 from tuberculosis, experienced a mystic connection: "all our diseases are phenomena of a heightened sensitivity that is about to be transformed into higher powers". His remarkable observation that "the more agonizing the pain, the more intense is the pleasure behind it", which borders on the masochistic, is similar to Nietzsche's experience: "I have never felt happier with myself than in the sickest periods of my life, periods of the greatest pain." He welcomed suffering as a goad to creativity.

These views culminate in the pages on suffering in Schopenhauer's "Parerga and Paralipomena",[54] so enjoyable in their clear-eyed pessimism. True to his nature, Schopenhauer sees a positive value in pain, because of the intensity of the sensation, and assigns a negative value to well-being, which he finds tedious and liable to turn into boredom. (I have not been able to console many of my patients with this argument.) Schopenhauer observes that we generally experience pain far beyond our apprehension, pleasure far beneath expectation. For anyone who thinks that enjoyment surpasses or at least balances pain he recommends comparing the feelings of a beast of prey devouring another animal to those of the victim! In sum, Schopenhauer considers that man needs suffering and pain to help keep him on a steady course, just as a ship needs ballast. Edvard Munch uses a similar metaphor: "Without illness and anxiety I would have been a rudderless ship", and there was plenty of both to direct his course (Fig. 24).

Suffering has also been extolled in music. While still a young man Gustav Mahler declared that pain was his sole consolation; consequently lamenting tones sound through much of his music. He concluded, however, that the ultimate goal in art always is relief from suffering and the rising above it.

Let us end on a lyrical note and listen to this thought, pronounced by two female poets; first by the youngest and mildest of the Brontë sisters, the submissive Anne, when, dying from tuberculosis, she collected strength in her *Psalm of Resignation*:

> With secret labour to sustain
> In humble patience every blow;
> To gather fortitude from pain
> And hope and holiness from woe.

The words are repeated in Emily Dickinson's pure and personal, slightly trembling timbre when she was threatened with blindness (see page 73):

> Must be a Woe—
> A loss or so—
> To bend the eye
> Best Beauty's way—
>
> My loss, by sickness—Was it Loss?
> Or that Ethereal Gain
> One earns by measuring the Grave—
> Then—measuring the Sun

5. G. Mahler, Facsimile, Symphony no. 5, first movement. The composer laments—"Klagend".

My studies of the lives of artists have led me to conclude that many have been influenced by disease and thus I understand the view of Kretschmer[36] that healthy, harmonious individuals often lack the spur that incites "the demoniac ones" to heights of genius.

An example of the latter is Lord Byron, who found some comfort in his disability, a club-foot, noting that "an addiction to poetry is very generally the result of 'an uneasy mind in an uneasy body'; disease or deformity have been the attendants of many of our best; Collins – mad, Pope – crooked, Milton – blind".

Thomas Mann claims that a close connection exists between disease and artistic creation. He lets a poet in the early novel *Royal Highness* explain: "My health is poor. I dare not say unfortunately, for I am convinced that my talent is inseparably connected with bodily infirmity." Although ironically a man who enjoyed good health, he says that "disease is a means of acquiring knowledge". Thus, the fundamental themes in two of his greatest works, *The Magic Mountain* and *Doctor Faustus*, are tuberculosis and syphilis, respectively – the two chief chronic infections of his time.

Medical surroundings during adolescence or a serious disease in the family can leave profound traces even in the work of healthy artists. As Gustave Flaubert's father was a doctor with the family apartment in the hospital precinct, the boy spent his childhood in a place of suffering and death[71]—The sights when he played in the dissecting room deeply influenced his sensibility and contributed to a premature pessimism about life. When he began to lose both hair and teeth at an early age, he commented that "one is hardly born before putrefaction sets in". Both Keats and Charlotte Brontë were well informed about tuberculosis from the fate of their families before they fell victims themselves and Edvard Munch has given us an unforgettable memory of his dying sister in the *Sick girl*.

By preventing other activity, disease may be a factor that favours artistic creation. Because of prostatic disease with painful urinary calculi Michel de Montaigne had to refrain from the travelling he loved and, retiring to his castle, he concentrated on his essays; the enforced exile gave him the distance from which he could observe human existence, free from all illusions. Likewise we are perhaps indebted for a wealth of good music to the disease, probably asthma, which made it impossible for Vivaldi to pursue a career in the ministry. He was ordained a priest, but, unable to celebrate mass, he instead became choir master and later was appointed musical director.

At the end of the last century, Henri Matisse had already entered the legal profession when disease changed his life. He became ill with appendicitis and as complications supervened he had to refrain from work for nearly a year! As a diversion he started to do some painting and became fascinated: " I discovered colour – not through other painters' work but from the way light revealed itself in nature. I had become possessed by painting and could not abstain". He soon launched on an artistic career, distinguished as much by keen intelligence and bold invention as by delicate sensitivity. If Matisse had lived in our days when appendicitis is treated with operation and cured in a week's time, he might well have become a prominent lawyer instead of a pioneer of modern art.

Later in life Matisse demonstrated that severe illness can leave deep traces even when the patient recovers. When he was in his seventies, Matisse developed cancer of the colon. He reluctantly agreed to an operation which was performed by no less than three of the most prominent French surgeons. The patient's life was saved, but he was gravely ill and greatly shaken. The wound became infected, probably because the strong-willed master refused changing of the bandage! As a result he acquired a bothersome large hernia of the scar which kept him partially bedridden for most of his remaining 13 years.

I had a conversation with him some years later while he was lying in bed with a cat on his feet, directing with a long stick how his large cut-outs should be pasted on the canvas. He explained how his illness had altered his attitude to life and art. He wished to fill the new life given him with as much happiness as possible. During his earlier years he had often, by dint of great pain and effort,

6. *H. Matisse, Decorative figure against ornamental background. Wrestling with new problems, the artist attains bold harmonies, never realized before.*

broken new paths in modern art (Fig. 6); now he wished
to allow himself the joy of treading these paths again, light
of heart and without effort. This state of mind is reflected
in his pictures. In many of his early works one can see
him wrestling with new problems. Over his later work
rest a happy air of repose and relaxed contentment (Fig. 7).
Matisse himself was so convinced of the beneficial radia-
tion of his colour and its power to heal, that he hung his
pictures around the beds of ailing friends.

*7. H. Matisse, Blue nude crouching.
The late cut-outs are based on a total
command of his artistic means. Their
playful lightness reveals another facet
of his fertile imagination and versatile
personality.*

24

Salient features of creative personality

Examples of diseases which exert a radical influence on the artist's work are to be found across the whole spectrum of pathology, mental as well as physical: "Every pain has its cry—health alone is mute."

The first question is whether artists are at all to be counted among the mentally normal, a question half answered by the saying, "there is no cure for genius". At any rate, the proportion of individuals with a borderline mental constitution in the schizoid or cyclothymic direction is high among great creators. Aberrant psychic traits which in ordinary people would seem morbid may add to the originality and fascination of artistic creation; they may even constitute its basis or origin. Present psychiatric opinion holds that psychosis does not generate artistic genius but at best liberates powers of the imagination. One is not a genius because one is mad – but it may help! August Strindberg's schizophrenic paranoia threw a ghastly reflection on his hated female figures. The excited visions that tormented van Gogh during his epileptic attacks gave intense colour to his late landscapes, and Handel's manic states provided him with extraordinary creative strength when he composed the *Messiah*.

There is certainly nothing average about great creators, who generally differ from us common mortals in a variety of ways. "A poet", says Søren Kierkegaard, "is an unhappy being whose heart is torn by secret sufferings, but whose lips are so strangely formed that when the sighs and the cries escape them, they sound like beautiful music".[35]

Like curious children great artists see everything with innocent eyes, as though for the first time; for Baudelaire, "genius is simply childhood, rediscovered by an act of will". He also said, with a metaphor that suits our theme, that "artists are always in a state of spiritual convalescence". They are distinguished by spells of exaltation, more lively associations, and sharper perception of human situations and peculiarities. They have, above all, an urge to seek new and personal means of expression, paths of communication with fellow beings who can appreciate their new creations and share their deepest feelings. This urge to deliver their message may find pathetic outlets. One of the greatest Swedish artists, Carl Hill, confined to his room by mental disease, threw his drawings out of the window to passers-by.

A true artist must be a pioneer and runs the risk of becoming a pathfinder without fans or followers. Some artists can be totally crushed by lack of appreciation and give up creative work; others, mentally stronger like Cézanne, will stubbornly continue their lonely road, far from the madding crowd.

Interestingly, this situation can prove disastrous if the artist suddenly evokes general acclaim. Mark Rothko found abrupt success intolerable after years of struggling to find a style of his own. With the typical self-depreciation of the melancholic, he feared that he was overrated, or at least misunderstood, and sank into depression and paranoia for which, as always, alcohol proved to be a poor remedy; suicide only, gave lasting relief.[52] He could contend with adversity but not with success.

The individuality of the artist is obvious. Even if one does not agree completely with Plato and call inspiration a "divine mania", it nevertheless often appears during a state of ecstasy. Resembling a source, springing from unconscious depths of the personality, it may rise to the surface in the dreams — or in daydreams. Not that art constantly and effortlessly flows from the mind. Flaubert would "rather die like a dog than to save a second by leaving a sentence before it is perfect". Thomas Mann stresses it, "The difference between an author and an ordinary individual is that the author has greater difficulties in expressing himself". Degas felt the same about the art of painting, "It is simple before one knows how, but difficult once one has learned".

George Sand tells about Chopin that his inspiration came on suddenly. While taking a walk, for instance, it would ring in his head and he had to hurry back to the piano to retain the musical idea on paper. Now, she says, a most heart-rending activity began. He would shut himself up in his room for days; he wept, paced back and forth, broke his pencils in pieces, changed a bar hundreds of times — erased it, wrote it over again — and toiled with a single page with desperate tenacity. Eventually, he might still settle for the original draft. (cp. Cézanne, fig. 31)

A work of art is art and work — art revealed through work unseen. Even when conceived in ardent passion and created with intense pleasure, art is usually born like other great works, with blood, sweat, toil and tears. It is simply that these alone do not suffice; if the artist loses the urge and ability for creation, he dries up and takes to repetition and mannerism. Instead of singing like a nightingale with flowing invention, he repeats, like a dove or a cuckoo, the same old melody with painful monotony. His work degenerates into an unenterprising form which "smells of ordinariness".

It remains a mystery why one artist's work touches our innermost core while another's leaves us cold and indifferent. Plato says that "he who approaches the temple of the Muses without inspiration in the belief that craftsmanship alone suffices will remain a bungler and his presumptuous poetry will be obscured by the songs of the maniacs". I dare to choose as examples de Chirico after his surrealistic period, Scott Fitzgerald after *The Great Gatsby* and Rossini, who for the last 25 years of his life only composed little pieces for his own amusement which he called sins of his old age. These artists resemble the lilacs in a Swedish poem, "they flower fleetingly and wither slowly". Those with lasting inspiration, like Milton, could then be compared to the roses in Anakreon's ode, "The pleasing old age of the roses retains the fragrance of youth".

There are many poignant expressions for the deep despondency that artistic sterility produces, often aggravated by painful pangs of conscience over mechanical repetition of ideas already expressed before, and better. It may lead to long periods of inactivity. George Gissing gives a heart-rending description in *New Grub Street*. This vocational illness, a state of chilling impotence, as opposed to the fever of compulsive creativity, may be acute and temporary or tragically incurable.

Even an author as resourceful as Joseph Conrad was afflicted. He once complained that "the work of the last three months makes a miserable show, — as for the quantity. And I have sat days and days. It is an impossible existence—there are moments when I think against my will that I must give up".[17]

Melville had to give up for good. He was one of those authors who depend on a foundation of personal experience to build their fiction and thus risk exhausting their material. In crowning his sea stories with *Moby Dick*, Melville had used up the last major portion of his artistic capital, his years at sea. In a letter to Hawthorne he deplores the treasure spent: "But I feel that I am now come to the inmost leaf of the bulb, and that shortly the flower must fall to the mould", and somewhat later he told the same friend that he "had pretty much made up his mind to be annihilated".

Artificial stimulation of creativity

We can easily understand how, in this predicament, the artist endeavours to freshen the withering lilac, how he tries to keep alive the waning inspiration by means of artificial stimulation. The Swiss artist Fuseli's recipe is really innocent: he ate raw meat in the evening in order to have splendid dreams which he then transformed into fantastic visionary images. Even more harmless was the stimulant used by Friedrich Schiller – the scent of rotting apples; this helped to evoke a mood of reverie and he therefore kept such apples in the drawer of his desk. This was not always sufficent – Goethe claims he can identify the passages Schiller wrote when he was tipsy – but he never became an alcoholic like so many other great artists.

The kindling of creative power that alcohol can ignite may lead into abuse and must then be dearly paid for later, when the glow is covered by ashes; like all other nerve poisons, alcohol ultimately destroys the activity of the mind. Under its influence Utrillo painted the most exquisite pictures of Paris, with subtle nuances in white, greys and greens. It is recounted that his relatives left him with a bottle of wine and a new canvas, returning later to fetch an empty bottle and a drunk artist, but also a fine painting, often a view of Montmartre, with its vibrant Parisian atmosphere (Fig. 8). As his dependence on alcohol increased, his powers were enfeebled and his means of expression diluted, as witness his later pictures, with their rather glaring, facile effects and faltering execution (Fig. 9). The deleterious effect is noticeable in many authors as well. Tennessee William's creative power

degenerated from the strong, original plays of his healthy middle age to the weak, murky ones of his last decades, when the abuse of alcohol gave both him and his work a crazy, outrageous turn.

Apart from alcohol, in the nineteenth century, opium was the drug most commonly relied upon, especially by poets, both for stimulating creative ability and for relief from external difficulties or internal upheaval. English Romanticism offers a number of examples. Coleridge saw the palace of Kubla Khan in a trance: "For he on honey-dew hath fed, And drunk the milk of Paradise."

Keats also tried the drug:

8. M. Utrillo, The windmills of Montmartre, 1912. A slight scent of alcohol does not noticeably vitiate the subtly rendered Paris atmosphere.

9. M. Utrillo, The windmills of Montmartre, 1953. Forty years later, wine and liquor have moved into the center, and the wings are cracked.

The continuous change in aesthetic convention is evident from the fact that some of my young friends prefer this late, awkward painting because of its more expressive approach as compared to the artistic refinement of the early version.

My heart aches, and a drowsy numbness pains
My sense, as though of hemlock I had drunk
Or emptied some dull opiate to the drains
One minute past and Lethe-wards had sunk.

He later abstained because of its dulling effect on the mind:

No, no, go not to Lethe,
— — — —
For shade to shade will come too drowsily
And drown the wakeful anguish of the soul.

In the mysterious twilight between reality and dreams "crowned with wreaths of poppies" we may also hear romantic music—in his *Symphonie Fantastique* Hector Berlioz resorts to the fiction of an opium dream when transforming the artist's sufferings and ecstasy into musical images. The sentimental programme provided by Berlioz could well have been conjured up by one of the Romantic poets: "A young composer of delicate sensitivity and passionate imagination has poisoned himself with opium in despair over unrequited love. As the dose was not lethal, it just threw him into a long sleep accompanied by bizarre visions where the spiritualized beloved, like a fixed idea, returns over and over again in a rapturous melody."

We know that Berlioz occasionally took strong medicine, probably containing narcotics, to relieve agonizing toothache but there is no indication that he ever used drugs to become intoxicated as De Quincey did.

This candid author of the *Confessions of an English Opium-Eater*[19] became a slave to the craving. As he, in his own words, was "upon such a theme not simply the best but surely the sole authority", he was able to give us a deep, eloquent and masterly narrative, both of the de-

lights and of the agonies of drug abuse. He says, not in
his defense — because the habit of eating opium was rather
common in his day and was not considered a vice — but as
an explanation that it was not "any search after pleasure
but mere extremity of pain" that first drove him into the
use of opium. He states that his pain was caused by
rheumatic toothache but from his description it is evident
that it was something worse, namely trigeminal neuralgia.

This disease is characterized by attacks of piercing pain
in the face, of such severity that they sometimes force
the victim into suicide. It is easily understandable that De
Quincey "began to use opium as an article of daily diet".
But the pain was not the main reason for his addiction, it
was rather his discovery of the effect of opium on his
spiritual life. He explains how he once tried to get relief
from his toothache by plunging his head into a basin of
cold water. This was a foolish action indeed since it is an
almost infallible way of provoking neuralgic attacks: "The
next morning, as I need hardly say, I awoke with excru-
ciating pains — from which I had hardly any respite for
about twenty days. On the twenty-first day — I went out
into the streets; rather to run away, if possible, from my
torments, than with any distinct purpose of relief. By
accident, I met a college acquaintance, who recommended
opium. Opium! Dread agent of unimaginable pleasure and
pain! I had heard of it as I had heard of manna or of
ambrosia, but no further."

De Quincey certainly manages to give the bleakest
background to his experience so that we should fully
appreciate his overwhelming revelation.

"It was a Sunday afternoon, wet and cheerless; and a
duller spectacle this earth of ours has yet to show than a
rainy Sunday in London. On my road homewards — I saw
a druggist's shop, where I asked for the tincture of opium.
Arrived at my lodgings I lost not a moment in taking the
quantity prescribed — and in an hour, Oh heavens! What a

revulsion, what a resurrection, from its lowest depths of the inner spirit! What an apocalypse of the world within me! That my pains had vanished, was now a trifle in my eyes; this negative effect was swallowed up in the immensity of these positive effects which had opened before me, in the abyss of divine enjoyment thus suddenly revealed. Here was a panacea for all human woes; here was the secret of happiness, about which philosophers had disputed for so many ages, at once discovered; happiness might now be bought for a penny and carried in the waistcoat-pocket; portable ecstasies might be corked up in a pint-bottle."

But the poor De Quincey came to know that divine enjoyment does not last forever. The blissful dreams eventually changed and assumed an increasingly horrible character, extorting from him "suspiria de profundis":

"The sense of space, and in the end the sense of time were both powerfully affected ... Space swelled, and was amplified to an extent of unutterable and self-repeating infinity. This disturbed me very much less than the vast expansion of time. I sometimes had feelings representative of a duration far beyond the limits of any human experience." He thus acquired a rare, tangible, sense of the relativity of space and time. The price was high:

"These changes in my dreams were accompanied by deep-seated anxiety and funereal melancholy ... I seemed every night to descend—not metaphorically, but literally to descend—into chasms and sunless abysses, depths below depths, from which it seemed hopeless that I could ever re-ascend ... The state of gloom which attended these gorgeous spectacles, amounting at last to utter darkness ... cannot be approached by words."

It has been at least approached by pictures—the magnificent engravings of Piranesi, *Carceri d'Invenzione*, convey the same feelings of desperate hopelessness. In gigantic, mystically boundless buildings with fantastic architecture, small figures lose themselves in massive flights of steps and staircases which lead nowhere—except when suddenly ending in dark space. The similarity in expression is no coincidence: Coleridge once described these imaginary prisons to De Quincey so vividly that we have no difficulty identifying the very plate (Fig. 10).

But the resemblance has deeper causes, indicating the similarity between states of depression from drug abuse and those of other origin. De Quincey no doubt recognized his own "deep-seated anxiety and funereal melancholy" in the somber spirit that created these pictorial "suspiria de profundis", sighs from the depths, and presumed that they must stem from "visions during the delirium of a fever". They rather result from a true manic-depressive tendency. "Piranesi dwelled on these prisons with such exuberance and frenzy that we have to look for their origin in the deepest sources of his nature, in the sombre passion which penetrates his personal life."[24] He was extremely irascible and disputes with comrades could end in physical assault; he even threatened the life of a doctor whom he thought had neglected his dying child!

In between he withdrew in sullen solitude, yelling to visitors that he, Piranesi, was unavailable. His youth was haunted by pathetic and funereal visions; thus he turned from studying models in the art academy to focus on the ill and crippled who exposed their misery in Italian churches. The lugubrious and magnificent imagination which devised the mature, late edition of the *Carceri*, among the most powerful engravings ever made, with their alarming depths and melancholic obscurity, was obviously depressive.[74] There are the morbid details reminiscent of Méryon's schizophrenic etchings (Fig. 20). Victor Hugo rightly talks about Piranesi's "black brain". The horrible, disquieting effect is enhanced by the fact that this mysterious and fantastic architecture is so rational—the endless staircases are solidly supported and the instruments of

10. G. B. Piranesi, *A prison of imagination, conveys a claustrophobic feeling of desperate hopelessness.*

11. *M. C. Escher, Hol en bol, 1955.*
Absurd architecture.

torture are technically perfect. It is the same kind of horror that Edgar Allan Poe experienced in his opium dreams
and made so real in his fantastic tales, for example *The Pit
and the Pendulum*.

The disorientation in space is repeated in M. C.
Escher's gruesome houses where the eyes get lost in all
directions and there is no telling what is in or out, up or
down. This artist exemplifies that one does not have to be
insane in order to create absurd works. The fact that he
was probably mentally healthy and handles his means
with a Northern rationality does not decrease the shocking effect of his art.

A recent addict to opium is the poet and artist Jean
Cocteau, who used the drug as an aid to recover mental
balance: "I preferred an artificial harmony to no harmony
at all." His self-portrait in *Journal d'une désintoxication*
vividly depicts the ordeal of this cure and how he was
helped by creativity (Fig. 12).

The intensely tragic interest in drugs other than opium and alcohol has made its impression on art, where these agents have been used in an attempt to extend the frontier of human experience and to sound hitherto impenetrable depths. In drug-induced hallucinations a sharpening of the sensations is combined with dissolution of their borders. Coloured visions may assume a tactile quality and sounds may be perceived as colours. This synesthesia of images

12. J. Cocteau, Désintoxication, 1929. The painful ordeal of weaning from opium is depicted in drawings "which became the faithful graph of the last stage", and in notes of frankness: "Sweat and bile precede some phantom substance which would have dissolved, leaving no other trace behind except a deep depression, if a fountain pen had not given it a direction, relief and shape.—After the cure came the worst moment, the worst danger, health with this void and an immense sadness. The doctors frankly hand you over to suicide".

yields important information about the correlations between art forms. Both Rimbaud and Théophile Gautier,
founders of the "Club des Hachichiens" in the middle of
the 19th century, thought they could actually hear the
sounds of colours – green, red, blue and yellow tones.
Gautier relates strange experiences during hashish intoxication: "It was as if I had been dissolved into nothing, so
absent and liberated from my Self, that disagreeable witness which haunts us everywhere, that I for the first time
in my life could form a conception of the angels and the
souls, emancipated from the body."

Baudelaire experienced the same excessive intensifi-
cation of vitality, of getting "high". Once during hashish

13. C. Baudelaire, Self portrait
drawn during marijuana intoxication. Strong sense of feeling
"high"—compared to the Vendôme column!

intoxication he drew a self-portrait (Fig. 13) that expresses very animatedly the feeling of being vastly superior—literally twice as tall as the Vendôme column! When sober, he suffered from disgust and void: "In order not to feel the horrible burden of Time which crushes one's shoulders and presses one to the ground, one must intoxicate oneself continually."

Henri Michaux has written poetry and painted under the influence of a hallucinogen, mescaline. In those pictures we see the external sensory world transformed and animated with monstrous beings (Fig. 14). They remind us of some of the etchings of Goya who knew that *When reason sleeps, monsters appear*. Even more striking is their resemblance to drawings by true schizophrenics like the Swedish artist Carl Hill (Fig. 15), which convinces us of

14. H. Michaux, Mescaline drawing. The surrounding world full of beasts and monsters.

15. C. F. Hill, The beasts and monsters as seen and drawn by the schizophrenic have an astounding resemblance to those drawn by Michaux under the influence of mescaline.

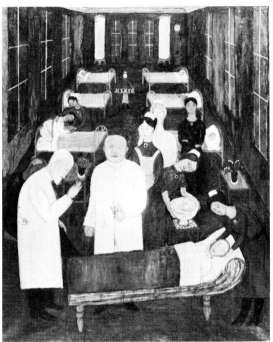

the close connection between this kind of intoxication and psychosis.

17. H. Linnqvist, The hospital ward has an anguishing atmosphere of disease and fever.

These artificial paradises, or rather hells, thus bring us imperceptibly to mental disease. The transition can be represented by a temporary condition, familiar to us all, the derangement of the senses from high fever. Artists have tried to express their delirious dreams; in *Hospital Ward* (Fig. 17) Hilding Linnqvist renders the anguishing atmosphere, smelling of antiseptics, while doctors and nurses do their rounds as observed in a trance. We are reminded of De Quincey's idea that Piranesi's prisons must stem from "visions during the delirium of fever".

40

Neuroses and psychosomatic disorders

The neuroses and psychosomatic disorders are of special interest to us as they strongly influence or even constitute the foundation of artistic creation. They vary greatly in character and degree. In their mildest form they may only consist of some fixed idea or of an exaggerated conception of ordinary corporeal reactions which get mistaken for disease. In their more severe form the emotional stress may give rise to an actual physical disorder like gastric ulcer or asthma. With their sensitive disposition artists easily fall victim to this kind of illness.

At the light end of the scale there is Piet Mondrian.[43] The lifestyle of this pioneer of puristic abstract art was marked by an obsessive orderliness; he was punctilious, even finical. These peculiarities distinguished everything he undertook. He was fond of dancing and danced elaborately, according to the rules, but his movements were rigid and angular. He kept his studio meticulously clean, never a grain of dust, everything white, sparse, immaculate. This personality trait had a direct bearing on his art. His colours were absolutely pure and finally reduced to the primary prismatic, red, yellow and blue. One has the impression that when he occasionally mixed white and black to a pleasing grey (Fig. 1) he felt that he was committing a daring compromise.

The strictly vertical and horizontal lines are subtly distributed according to some subconscious plan and the rectangles are balanced with a pious, transcendent harmony of which he himself was aware; he was convinced that he was delivering a special message.

Gustav Mahler's fear of death and hope of resurrection,

which flow as a mighty undercurrent in his music, had a medical source.[15] His doctor had early diagnosed a heart murmur due to a slight valvular defect, and unheedingly cautioned him against physical exertion, a warning that could give trepidation to anybody. Of Mahler it made an anguished hypochondriac. According to his wife,[41] his reaction was extremely neurotic: "We avoided strenuous walks owing to the ever-present anxiety about his heart. Once we knew he had valvular disease ... we were afraid of everything. He was always stopping on a walk to feel his own pulse; and he often asked me ... to listen to his heart and hear whether the beat was clear, or rapid, or calm ... His steps and pulse beats were numbered and his life a torment." One may surmise that Mahler found refuge from his fear in his music, that he turned his apprehension into his very personal tones and harmonies (see pages 20 and 121).

Marcel Proust's intense interest in and vivid memories of even the smallest details of ordinary life, which constitute the substance of his great autobiographical novel *A la recherche du temps perdu*, were also responsible for his neurotic disposition when they concerned his bodily sensations. His sickly disposition ever since childhood caused his parents concern. The experience of unceasing medical care generated an absorption in disease, his own and others, evident throughout the novel, and provided him with the abundance of metaphors, often astonishingly initiated in the medical domain, that is so characteristic of his literary style: "He did not release her, instead he waited like a surgeon awaits the end of the patient's paroxysm, which has interrupted his operation, before he continues".

After the death of his mother, on whom he had a strong infantile dependence, Proust gradually withdrew from social engagements. His allergic asthma got worse and he increased the intake of potent drugs–opium, veronal and heroin—in a disastrous attempt for relief. His habits became increasingly nocturnal and during long working hours in his bedroom, lined with cork to exclude noise, the great novel developed in an almost autonomic fashion; his deteriorating health made him fear that he would not be able to complete his task.

Proust says himself that "Everything great in the world is created by neurotics. They have composed our master-pieces. We enjoy delightful music, beautiful paintings and thousands of small miracles, but we don't consider what they have cost their creators in sleepless nights, rashes, asthma, epilepsy—and, worst of them all, fear of death." When this eventually drew near, he observed: "A stranger has taken her abode in my mind.—I was surprised at her lack of beauty. I had always thought Death beautiful, how otherwise should she get the better of us?" George Pickering, [51] in his essay *Creative Malady*, suggests that Proust, realizing that creativity is a solitary activity, took refuge in his disease in order to procure the seclusion necessary for superhuman achievement.

The same had probably been the case with Flaubert after his father had sent him to law school: his disgust and boredom promoted the onset of epilepsy that secured his return home to the dreaming, reading and writing which engrossed him. After his father's death, when the fits had served their purpose, they conveniently subsided.

An example of how neurosis may turn into mental obsession is provided by the Swedish scientific author and professor of theology, Samuel Ödman, who in his youth was one of Linnaeus' favourite pupils. He so feared catching cold that even the threat of a draft made him shiver. He admits himself that "your otherwise sensible friend becomes demi-maniac the moment he grasps the doorknob". For safety's sake he took to his bed at the age of 43 and remained there for forty years, until he exchanged it for the most secluded one.

18. J. G. Sandberg, Portrait of Samuel Ödman. In order to protect himself from drafts and chills, the neurotic author stayed in bed for 40 years, dressed in his coat and covered with blankets. "Only in his youth had he lived in the bosom of Nature. He took the picture of it with him inside the four walls that then became his outer world—as fresh as if it was from yes-terday." From his miserable confine-ment he exerted an important influ-ence on the international world of learning of his time.

Mental diseases

Words will avail the wretched mind to ease
and much abate the dismal black disease. (Horace)

The connections between mental disease and art have
such a vide scope that they form a complete science,
known as psycho-iconography. I shall give a few samples.

Mental disease exerts a profound influence on artistic
activity. Pictures produced by the mentally ill have
provided fundamental insight into certain manifestations of mental disease, and in certain cases can even help
us to reach a *diagnosis*. Moreover, artistic activity and the
creation of pictures often have an excellent *therapeutic*
effect.[6] There are, for instance, distressing conditions
where as a result of mental disease the patient is apathetic
and withdrawn, and lacks the ability to communicate with
other people. If the patient can be induced to paint, the
barrier may be removed so that he re-establishes contact
with the environment, a change that he often perceives as
an intense feeling of relief. Here is one of the links between psychiatric art and normal art. It is a fact that here,
too, one of the most important inducements is a desire of
the artist to communicate with his fellow men, to obtain
a sense of close personal contact, and to deliver himself
from suffering by creating. Heinrich Heine said it in
verse:

> Disease may well have been the ground
> In full for that creative urge,
> Creation was my body's purge,
> Creating I've grown sane and sound

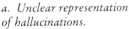

19. Anonymous. Schizophrenic drawings by a mute and apathetic patient.

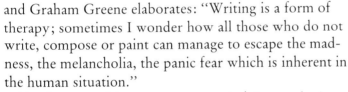

a. Unclear representation of hallucinations.

b. With improving capacity, the hallucination of a monster becomes clear.

c. Split personality expressed by half-erased face.

and Graham Greene elaborates: "Writing is a form of therapy; sometimes I wonder how all those who do not write, compose or paint can manage to escape the madness, the melancholia, the panic fear which is inherent in the human situation."

To give a case history as an example:[1] An apathetic woman stayed isolated, with no contact at all with her surroundings. When given a pencil and paper she made a drawing (Fig. 19a) which is somewhat difficult to understand. According to the specialist's interpretation, the patient has drawn a picture of herself, torn by some peculiar figures that she sees in her hallucinations. She continued to draw and in this way opened up her mind still more, so that it became easier to understand what she experienced.

In the next picture (19b) she was able to represent more clearly both herself and the evil spirits that threaten her during her hallucinations. A patient who has been induced in this way to reveal to her physicians what is going on in her mind will often be more accessible for treatment and will then improve. In the last drawing (19c) she has made a self-portrait but with half of the face erased; this is common for persons with her illness, schizophrenia. The patient senses a "splitting" of the personality and illustrates this with the double face. The similarity to some of Picasso's portraits is evident, and throws light on how art can disclose obscure phenomena in the emotional life of man.

A number of great artists have been frankly insane. One of the outstanding etchers of the last century, Charles Méryon, became schizophrenic and went through all the stages to the final mental breakdown.[40] In his famous series *Eaux-fortes sur Paris* we have the rare opportunity of following the progress of this psychosis and its relation to creativity in the works of a great artist. Even the prints that preceded obvious signs of disease reveal a schizophrenic personality—and this might account for their fascinating originality. Victor Hugo saw it: "The work of Méryon is pervaded by the breath of the infinite; the etchings are more than pictures—they are visions—his plates live, radiate light and seem even to think." His greatest work dates from the time when his psychosis was beginning to show symptoms. The remarkable etching *La Morgue* (Fig. 20) depicts a gloomy corner of the city with an oppressive atmosphere and morbid details. Méryon finally was confined to an asylum and his talent deteriorated—though with some lucid intervals. During one of these he created *Ministère de la Marine* (Fig. 21), where his original genius is evident in the imposing architectural majesty, while his deranged, dismal imagination produced monsters in the sky.

In two paintings by an eminent Swedish artist, Ernst Josephson, we have another opportunity of comparing artistic greatness and its change under the influence of mental disease. One of the pictures was painted while he was in sound health; the other, somewhat later, when he had become schizophrenic.

From Josephson's last summer in good health we have

20. C. Méryon, *The morgue. Morbid details, such as a corpse being
fished out of the Seine, suggest a schizophrenic personality.*

21. C. Méryon, *In fully developed schizophrenia the artist
actually sees, and can depict, the monsters appearing in the sky.*

22. E. Josephson, The artist painted his beloved niece in a sunny glade shortly before he became insane and slid into darkness.

the painting of a young girl in the woods, a Nordic impressionism in which the soft French verdure has been replaced by the somber fir trees (Fig. 22). The sunny glade has an oriental richness of colour. The spontaneous naive delight strikes us even though it is still kept in check by tight artistic reins—as is the poem from the same time which he wrote for his much loved niece, the model for the picture.

Clad in boots and blue jacket
I could wander through the grass where the wild
Flowers spread their perfume.
There stood my pine, my ash, my birch with its tender
    leaves.
All was as in years gone by. Oh! how happy I was!
My ant-hill, my frogs, my angling worms in the earth,
My dragon-fly, my butterfly, my sun in all its golden
    splendour.

The deep impression that the disease made on Josephson's personality is discernible both in his art and in his letters. The normal mental inhibitions were dissolved and he lost control over his means of expression. But at the same time the restraints on his creative powers were also relaxed, and these erupted with enormous force, uncontrolled and uninhibited; of the measured impressionist the disease made a savage expressionist. The picture of his uncle, a stage manager at the Royal Theatre in Stockholm (Fig. 23), is reminiscent in its darkly splendid tonal scale of the late works of Rembrandt. Josephson himself best articulates his state of mind in a letter to an artist friend, where he suggests that they should take a voyage together:

> There we will let our brushes dance in a way unknown before in Sweden. Here I haven't a single tube of colour to squeeze. Let us spite Heaven and Hell from our palates – if need be paint on the same canvas with hands and feet. The waves will dance in our pictures, the clouds float across the skies and the wind stir the grass and twigs.

The idea of painting on the same canvas with hands and feet was revolutionary at that time—today such extravagance is generally accepted. Miró, Jackson Pollock and Tapiès used the technique and Yves Klein painted with the whole body!

When Josephson thus with a violent, unbridled passion, under the influence of his insanity, lets colour and emotion take precedence over exact drawing and reason, he anticipates European expressionism; having no immediate followers, he did not pioneer it. The one who resembles him most is Edvard Munch, whose work also was influenced by a morbid, probably schizophrenic state of mind. In *The Shriek* (Fig. 24) the great Norwegian master lets a tormented figure, rendered with burning colours

50

and agitated strokes, reveal his innermost feelings of horrible anxiety and of insecurity in his human relations.

During Vincent van Gogh's last and most creative years, his artistic powers were influenced and liberated by an unusual kind of epilepsy with crises of terrible anxiety, confusion and agression, sometimes intensified by absinthe intoxication. Once, during a delirious phase after

23. E. Josephson, The stage director, painted during mental disease in which impetuous feelings overpower controlled drawing. "Not until Joseph went mad did he find his right mind", one of his artist friends observed.

24. E. Munch, *The shriek, a violent, unbridled expression of anguish: "I was ill and tired—I stood there, watching the fjord—I felt as if a shriek went through nature—I thought I heard a shriek"*.

threatening to kill his friend Gauguin, he cut off the lobe of his ear and presented it to a prostitute. The result of this outburst is directly visible in a self-portrait with a bandage round the head (Fig. 25). Between the crises, van Gogh had what is called *hypergraphia*, compulsive exuberant artistic activity – it is to this symptom of his disease that we owe an overwhelming number of brilliant paintings, some of them created in a single day!: "I toil like one possessed, in a mute frenzy, more than ever. I fight with all my strength to master my art and tell myself that success would be the best lightning rod for my disease. — My brushes run as fast between my fingers as the bow over a violin". In a letter from his last summer he wrote: "I am painting immense expanses of wheat beneath

25. V. van Gogh, Self portrait with bandage after he had cut off part of his ear.

troubled skies, and I have not hesitated to express sadness, extreme solitude." In the final picture, *The Wheatfield* (Fig. 26), the extreme traits of his personality combine in a harrowing epitome: the manic component is reflected in the tempestuous, whirling brush strokes, the anxiety in the flock of black birds which incarnate the dismal thoughts that were soon to drive him to suicide.

Two composers who also alternately enjoyed and suffered manic and depressive tendencies, Handel and Schumann, had in common with van Gogh an astonishing ease and fluency of creation during their manic phases. Handel composed the *Messiah* during three weeks of hectic activity: "I thought I saw all heaven before me, and the Great God himself", and Schumann conceived and completed in six days the *Kreisleriana*, his most intimately subjective composition, the summit of musical romanticism. Writing to his beloved Clara Wieck, Schumann comments: "I have finished a series of new pieces which I call *Kreisleriana*. It is completely dominated by you and your thoughts and I want to dedicate them to you, and to no one else.* Then you will smile with your characteristic gracefulness and you will recognize it. My music seems so wonderfully composed, so simple, coming right from the heart. It is fantastic, mad, indeed awful; you will be astonished when you play it. Otherwise, right now, it often seems to me that I am going to burst from music!"

Even if Clara recognized the intonation, she was surely astonished at how agitated and, at times, disharmonic it was, and worried that it might not be appreciated. Like van Gogh, Schumann had expressed simultaneously in a single work the extreme duality of his nature, both the melancholy and the violent passion. In this fantastic and audacious composition, wild and demonic movements succeed tender and meditative ones with a fury that sur-

---

* He finally dedicated them to Chopin!

54

prised Schumann himself, enraptured by an unbridled and wayward inspiration. The presentiment that he had expressed in his letter to Clara proved true and *Kreisleriana* was premonitory – the composer died insane.

Friedrich Nietzsche's insanity, caused by tertiary syphilis, terminated in mental breakdown and general paralysis.[18] Symptoms of madness are increasingly evident in his last works and it is sometimes difficult to discern where health ends and disease takes over; what role, for example, did syphilis play in the begetting of "der Übermensch"? The triumphant self-assertion which characterizes the incipient madness of his last work is evident in this quotation from the somewhat bizarre *Ecce Homo*: "Genius is *conditioned* by dry air, by a pure sky—that is to say, by rapid metabolism, by the possibility of constantly procuring for oneself, great, even enormous quantities of strength." Nietzsche thus is one of those cases where severe mental symptoms in life and work are caused by organic changes in the brain.

26. *V. van Gogh, In the wheatfield there are simultaneous maniacal manifestations in the tempestuous brush strokes and depressive traits with the threatening sky and the ominous black birds.* "*The crisis caught me out in the field when I was painting on a stormy day – I felt like a coward from anxiety. – Everything must be forced to a peak in order to arrive at those loud-yellow tones*".

Congenital malformations

Turning to actual physical illness, it is natural to start with the inherited disorders, the congenital malformations. Man has an instinctive loathing for these and they tend to cause aversion in fellow-beings and an irrational sense of shame in the victim. These unfortunates, then, sometimes react with bashful resignation but more often with revolt and extreme efforts to compensate, often with artistic creation. In Sir Francis Bacon's words "Whosoever hath anything fixed in his person that doth induce contempt, hath also a perpetual spur in himself to rescue and deliver himself from scorn, therefore all deformed persons are extreme bold."

Charles Lamb noticed this in Daniel Defoe, who lacked external ears: "Neither have I incurred, nor done anything to incur, with Defoe, that hideous disfigurement, which constrained him to draw upon assurance to feel 'quite unabashed' and at ease upon that article."

An excess of lineaments is equally disfiguring. Nicolai Gogol was endowed with a huge, mobile nose which made him a laughingstock. He compensated by making comedy of his unseemly snout. In one of his stories the nose of a conceited bureaucrat mysteriously disappears and is discovered parading down the street!

The most sublime compensation conceivable is that achieved by Michelangelo. Saddened by his distorted nose, broken during a fight in childhood, the vain artist proved, by assigning the same fault to one of his divine Madonnas, that this was not incompatible with wonderful beauty.

22b. The "Manchester Madonna", ascribed to Michelangelo, detail. The National Gallery, London.

The fact that the painter pictured the Madonna with a broken nose that bears a strong likeness to that of Michelangelo supports the attribution to this master.

56

In the early eighteenth century *The Hunchback Song*, a comic glorification of this deformity, was very popular. Its author had an enormous hump but was the first to make fun of it; hunchbacks have always had a reputation for gaiety and wit, that is why they often became jesters. On the first night of his song, the author gave a big dinner — but only hunchbacks were invited; quite a party it must have been with all the guests bent on their food!

A perfect example of the profound effect of a malformation on both life and personality, thereby influencing creative work, we find in Lord Byron, whose misshapen foot, in his own words, was his "curse of life". Byron was intensely sensitive to the deformity, which he tried to conceal in every way, and any allusion to it would drive him into a furious rage, especially when made by a female. His own mother did not hide her disgust with the child and had him subjected to extremely painful treatment by a quack, who for quite some time tried in vain to redress the deformed foot. Byron's wounded pride was decisive in forming the arrogant independence in his character and brought forth the achievements of his youthful genius. Any doubts about the connection are dispelled by his own words:

> Deformity is daring.
> It is its essence to o'ertake mankind
> By heart and soul and make itself the equal—
> Ay the superior of the rest. There is
> A spur in its halt movements to become
> All that the others cannot, in such things
> As still are free to both, to compensate
> For stepdame Nature's avarice at first.

Byron passed his life in courting agitation and difficulties, and in his fiction he has a preference for rebels like Don Juan and Cain who are aloof, solitary and endowed with an acute sensitivity to pain. Cain's career followed a By-

27. Santeul, The Hunchback, Facsimile.
"Long ago I discovered why Punch thought it such fun to have a hunch."

ronic pattern: a malcontent, isolated from his fellow men, he rebelled against authority and became an outcast.

In his contempt for mankind there is only one person for whom Byron feels unbounded love and respect, his half-sister (and half-bride?), Augusta Leigh:

> Though I feel that my soul is deliver'd
> To pain—it shall not be its slave.
> There is many a pang to pursue me:
> They may crush, but they shall not contemn—
> They may torture, but shall not subdue me—
> 'T is of *thee* that I think—not of them.
> Though human, thou didst not deceive me,
> Though woman, thou didst not forsake.

Toulouse-Lautrec, who was even more conspicuously deformed than Byron, had little choice but to resign and withdraw. As a member of the nobility, he would certainly have been assigned a military career, had it not been for the aberration in his bodily development with very short legs and a deformed head, evident in numerous self portraits (Fig. 29). He conformed to his situation by seeking

28. H. de Toulouse-Lautrec, In his self portraits the artist shows his short legs and deformed face.

his company among prostitutes and his motives in the brothels, where his social level was of no consequence and his appearance ignored.

To vindicate himself despite his deformity he took the motto: "Paint, drink and love" and ended up a great painter, an alcoholic with attacks of delirium tremens, and a syphilitic. Towards the end of his life he was bothered by hallucinations. Vuillard was an eye-witness: "Lautrec was too proud to submit to his lot, a physical freak, an aristocrat cut off from his kind by his grotesque appearance. He found an affinity between his own condition and the moral penury of the prostitute. He may have seemed cynical, but if so it was from an underlying despair ... I was always moved by the way in which Lautrec changed his tone when art was discussed. He who was so cynical and so foul-mouthed on all other occasions became completely serious. It was a matter of faith with him ... Poor Lautrec! I went to see him one day, just after he had been put in a home in Neuilly. He hadn't long to live. He was a dying man, a wreck. His doctor had told him to 'take exercise', so he had bought a gymnasium horse — Lautrec, who couldn't even get his foot on the pedals! A cruel irony — and yet it symbolized his whole life!"

There is a notable instance of physical affliction which actually benefitted artistic performance. One of the greatest violinists of all times, Paganini, "Demon of Fiddlers," was marked by disease. Rarely has a great artist worked in such a miserable condition. There was no end to his sufferings — he was plagued by tuberculosis and syphilis, osteomyelitis of the jaw, diarrhea, hemorrhoids, urinary retention and infection. The diseases and the treatment he received gave him an increasingly strange and emaciated appearance; the mercury prescribed for his syphilis made him lose his teeth and gave his skin a peculiar coloration.

29. D. Maclise, A drawing of the violin virtuoso Paganini demonstrates the hyperflexible joints, typical of his congenital disease—look at the left thumb which could be bent back to the extent of touching the little finger!

But the most remarkable feat in his pathology was a congenital disorder, the Ehlers-Danlos' syndrome, which at the same time constituted the basis for his violinistic virtuosity. The condition is characterized by laxity of the connective tissue and an excessive flexibility of the joints. This enabled Paganini to perform the astonishing double-stoppings and roulades for which he was famous. His wrist was so loose that he could move and twist it in all directions. Although his hand was not disproportional he could thus double its reach and play in the first three positions without shifting.

This kind of disorder which usually is detrimental to the individual became in Paganini's instance artistically beneficial—it was "a blessing in disguise." And what a disguise it was! From descriptions by contemporaries we learn that his peculiar habitus, the strange, angular bendings of his body and a lividly corpse-like face gave him a freakish appearance, strangely provocative of laughter. This impression was, however, instantly suppressed when the master set the violin beneath his chin and began to play: the first stroke of his bow was like an electric spark that gave him new life. "He threw the bow on the strings and ran up and down the scales with marvelous rapidity, the cadences rippling out from beneath his fingers like strings of pearls."

His trills of ease were trills of disease. Liszt wrote in his obituary that "the wonderful meeting of such a mighty talent with circumstances so adaptable to an apotheosis will remain a singularity in the history of art..."

Old age, debility and degeneration

Continuing now with bodily complaints, I shall turn to the opposite side of life and proceed with the most common one, the condition that we are all bound to endure if we are permitted to go on living, namely old age. A few, like Milton, Titian and Verdi, continue forcefully into late years, but for most, failing strength and increasing infirmity render work more difficult and cause apprehension that one's life-work will not be achieved.

Not many of us are as stoic as Dr. Samuel Johnson pretended to be when he remarked that the prospect of being hanged concentrates the mind wonderfully, or as François Villon, who had good reasons to fear that fate and thus expected that "the halter soon would teach his neck how much his bottom weighed".

No, for most of us death still has its sting and we feel, with de La Rochefoucauld, that there are two things we cannot contemplate with a steady eye: the sun and death. Even Dr. Johnson's stoicism was affected: "No rational man can die without apprehension." While it is a consolation to know that we share ultimate annihilation with all our fellow beings, and even hope "to pass away in peace", we will not escape our fate. Death shall ultimately tear us all asunder as wild animals rend their victims but it is the sensitive artist who most vividly can fancy the hot and stinking breath of the beast as it overpowers us.

The sudden threat of death may completely shatter creative power. This was the case with Theodor Storm.[32] This author developed cancer of the stomach and requested that his doctor reveal the situation "as man to man", but the rather naïve author had overestimated his mental strength and collapsed on hearing the truth. To help him, his brother called in a consultant who knowingly lied that the disease was innocuous. Storm believed him without hesitation, rallied and spent an excellent summer, crowning his career with a classic work, *Der Schimmelreiter*, for which we thus have to thank a merciful fraud. But the grace was short and the vision that he once had fancied became real:

> So strangely weird the world becomes
> and slowly all your hope deserts you
> until you know at last – at last
> that mortal shafts have struck you.

Kafka makes us understand how deserted and insecure a patient may feel when left in ignorance or deceit. From the sanatorium where he died two months later, he wrote to a friend: "Verbally I don't learn anything definite, since in discussing tuberculosis everybody drops into a shy, evasive, glossy-eyed manner of speech." I believe that Storm would have regained mental balance, even knowing the truth, if he had received the right support.

When shadows fall over the road, thoughts—and hence output—increasingly concern the shortness of life and its vanity. During his last years, Eugène Delacroix was fighting weariness, weakness and a feeling of incapability as he endeavoured to conclude his most demanding task—the paintings in St. Sulpice. In *Jacob wrestling with the angel* (Fig. 30), he probably depicts his own situation of man struggling with his fate.

Paul Cézanne, the lone pioneer on a new road in art (Fig. 31), became increasingly weak and infirm with diabetes towards the end of his life and understood that his days were numbered: "I glimpse the promised land, but shall I get there, or shall I end up like the leader of the

30. E. Delacroix, Jacob wrestling with the angel, is man, struggling with his fate, a losing battle. A sentence by the sorely afflicted Scott Fitzgerald, written shortly before his death, makes a fitting caption. He concludes that "life is essentially a cheat and its conditions are those of defeat, . . . the redeeming things are not 'happiness and pleasure' but the deeper satisfactions that come out of struggle."

Hebrews?" Only a few days before his death he wrote to his son: "I continue working with pains, but finally something will come out of it, and that is all that matters, I believe." In his late paintings, it is skulls that replace his beloved apples in the new harmony of the spheres. Compared to the luminous character of paintings from the 'nineties, the colours are more somber, the harmony is in the minor key and the feeling is deeply tragic.

A similar development is even more obvious in the late works of Mark Rothko. With failing health, death itself became an obsession and is the principal theme of the murals in the Rothko chapel in Houston where light and life fade away in the almost black purple.

When the ageing Haydn found it impossible to complete his last quartet he published two movements, adding these words: "All my strength is gone, I am old and feeble". He even put them on his visiting cards to escape further demands on his ability.

In other artists we may find that the body's decline is accompanied by impoverishment of the mind, with extinction of the creative flame. For every year that passes, one or more strings of the soul snap and the tone becomes

31. P. Cézanne, His apples form a new harmony of the spheres.

32. P. Cézanne, In his old age, the artist replaces the apples with skulls, the symbol of vanity.

"He actually worked without joy, it seems, in a constant rage, in conflict with every single one of his paintings, none of which seemed to achieve what he considered the most indispensable thing, La réalisation" *(Rilke).*

thinner. A remaining note which previously enriched the harmony then produces a shrill dissonance.

The erotic tone – often merely intimated by a simple wavy line (Fig. 33) – that endowed the works of the young Picasso with human fullness could occasionally turn into boyish mischief, but it is only later, when this note is struck alone, monotonously, by the ageing man that it degenerates into pornography. He now easily confuses the eager artistic exploration of the curves, creases and crevices of the female body with the latent physical

33. P. Picasso, The young artist contemplates his model with tenderness and discretion.

lust for penetration (Fig. 34) and the spiritual vision gives way to obscene contemplation with the artist as voyeur.

Even in senility, Picasso preserved a powerful faculty of artistic expression, which makes some of his works summits of erotic art. One would rather ascribe to him the comment that he "painted with his penis", than to the chaste Renoir who allegedly made the statement. For the latter this seems to be much too coarse a way of indicating the elementary eroticism which was the undercurrent of his inspiration.

Renoir was one of those fortunate artists whose creative powers endure into old age even when this is accompanied by more pronounced infirmities. In them one often finds a longing for the happiness of earlier years. In middle age Renoir was for a time the victim of an ambition that one sometimes finds among artists, namely to reach beyond their ability. In his efforts to adapt to the classical ideal he was liable to be dry and cold. But in his advancing years he recovered his personality. Despite painful old-age arthritis, which obliged him to tape cotton to the palm of his hand so as to be able to hold the brush, as we see in a

34. P. Picasso, With increasing senile eroticism, the ageing master gets seduced by his own art and makes shameless advances to his subjects, somewhat distracting his contemplation—and that of his spectators.

self-portrait, he painted pictures that radiate youthful joy, and took delight in representing children, young girls and the flowers of spring (frontispiece).

The ageing Montaigne gives us a fitting caption: "Youth sees ahead, old age looks back: was not this the significance of Janus' double face? Let the years drag me along, if they will, but then backwards! As long as my eyes can discern that fair expired season of life, I shall now and then turn them that way. Though youth escapes from my blood and my veins, I shall at least not tear the image of it from my memory."

One has a feeling that Renoir, too, fondly treasured the memory of his youth, in a healthy, vital way, and we note the absence of constraint in his adaptation of a direct landscape to a classical composition. His colour scale also becomes brighter–possibly because of impaired sight, but certainly also intentionally from a desire to achieve a warmer tone. In this connection must be mentioned the

35. A. Renoir, In this self portrait, the artist shows how cotton was wound around his arthritic fingers to enable him to hold the brush.

36. P. Klee, The artist, struggling to create in spite of severe disease which crippled his hands and impeded his wielding of the crayon. (See page 114.)

hypothesis that Renoir's arthrosis was an occupational disease, caused by poisoning from his pigments. As his light colours needed the heavy lead, he might have paid for his radiant light, the delight of us all, with his own health.

The same explanation has been given for Dufy's rheumatoid arthritis—but the medical history of this artist differed from that of Renoir in two important respects: his disease had started earlier and was even more disabling than Renoir's and it was remarkably improved by medical treatment; in the words of his doctor,[30] "The medical story of Raoul Dufy represents one of those rare instances in which a medical advance is made at exactly the right

37a. R. Dufy, Rigid lines in drawing and handwriting caused by stiff joints.

37b. R. Dufy, After treatment with anti-inflammatory hormones the lines are relaxed and the mood relieved.

time to salvage creative functioning in an important person and thereby enrich our heritage".

This singular circumstance enables us to study not only how Dufy's art was crippled by his disease, as was his body, but also how it reverted to its original greatness and perhaps even progressed further through medical treatment. This happened when Dufy was 73 years of age, completely infirm and immobilized after fifteen years of disease. His drawing had become laboured and his lines as rigid as his joints.

The artist now became one of the first patients to be treated with the new hormones, ACTH and cortisone, which counteract inflammatory processes. The result was dramatic: within a few days the patient became mobile and the movements of all his joints increased. For the first time in several years he was able to squeeze his paint tubes unassisted. After six weeks Dufy was enjoying life anew, alert and active. The effect on his work is evident when one compares his handwriting as well as his pictures painted before and after treatment, when his art flourished afresh and he again became master of his means. These drugs often arouse euphoria and Dufy sensed it; he named one of the magnificent flower-pieces *Cortisone*!

Was there even a renewed progress in his creative ability? The artist thought so: "Everything continues to go well for me. Whether because of cortisone or hormones I don't know, but I am now painting themes that I studied when I was young and which naturally did not satisfy me at that time. To works constructed in the Cézanne manner I have added pure and imaginary colours, which I have been searching in vain to do for more than 30 years. Does this represent a renaissance or a swan song of Fauvism, or is it an error of my misled senses, induced by the excitement of a successful work?"

38. El Greco, At the burial of the Conde de Orgaz the terrestrial humans are of normal size, whereas the celestial residents are elongated, which demonstrates that the distorsion is not a sign of eye affection but a means of enhancing the artistic expression.

Defects of sight and hearing

The artist naturally is highly dependent on sensory perception, especially sight and hearing. These are often diminished in advanced age, but they can also be impaired by disease. Of the changes in the sensory organs, one would imagine that those involving the eyes would affect the artist most deeply. With failing sight, Degas turned from painting to sculpture when he found that in modeling he could rely more on his tactile sense. The colour-blindness of Whistler and Léger can be discerned in their painting.

The most usual and convincing manifestation of eye affections is perhaps that resulting from senile cataract, or opacity of the lens, which leads a painter to use a colour scale that is shifted towards red, so as to recover the balance as we can see it in Monet (tailpiece, p. 143).

It is well established that abnormal sight was not what caused El Greco to elongate his figures.[29] As he saw nature and his paintings with the same eyes, the effect of any astigmatism would have been neutralized. Equally important is the aesthetic evidence. In several of El Greco's paintings the proportions are elongated in some places, normal in others, indicating that he used distortion purely for artistic reasons, to communicate his emotion. This is obvious in one of the great paintings of all time, *Burial of the Conde de Orgaz*. In the terrestrial region, where the corpse is being lowered into the ground, everybody is of ordinary human stature. Above, where heaven opens dramatically, even the soul of the deceased, kneeling before God, has the ethereal and ecstatic, elongated shape of the celestial residents (Fig. 38).

Since antiquity, loss of sight has been related to the gift of prophecy and poetry. Homer tells us about Demodo-cus, the "sacred master of heavenly song":

> Loved by the Muse was the bard: but she
> Gave him of good and of evil
> Reft was the light of his eyes, but with
> Sweetest song he was dowered.

The sweetest song seems often to be a sufficient conso-lation – Milton composed *Paradise Regained* after he had lost his eyesight. In a famous sonnet

> When I consider how my light is spent
>   Ere half my days in this dark world and wide,

he refers to his blindness as "a mild yoke":

> "Doth God exact day-labor, light denied?"
>   I fondly ask. But Patience, to prevent
> That murmur, soon replies, "God doth not need
>   Either man's work or his own gifts. Who best
>   Bear his mild yoke, they serve him best. – – –

He still at times felt heavy laden. Totally blind when marrying his second wife, he never saw her but in fleeting dreams. When she died, two years later, after childbirth, he laments his double loss in a last, sublime line:

> Methought I saw my late espoused Saint – – –
>   – such, as yet once more I trust to have
>   Full sight of her in Heaven without restraint,
> Came vested all in white, pure as her mind:
>   Her face was veil'd, yet to my fancied sight,
>   Love, sweetness, goodness, in her person shin'd
> So clear, as in no face with more delight.
>   But O, as to embrace me she inclin'd
>   I wak'd, she fled, and day brought back my night.

72

The blind poet found a brother in misfortune in the Bible, Samson Agonistes, eyeless in Gaza. "O loss of sight, of thee I most complain!" the giant laments. At the time he was composing the oratorio to Milton's text, Handel was also losing his eyesight, and could enter with a similar vehemence into the feelings of the blinded Samson:

> "O dark, dark, dark, amid the blaze of noon,
> Irrecoverably dark, total Eclipse
> Without all hope of day!"

To all three, Samson, Milton and Handel, light, now a lost paradise, was the prime of creation:

> "O first created Beam, and thou great Word,
> Let there be light, and light was over all;
> Why am I thus bereaved thy prime decree?"

When those in the audience who knew the story heard this song, they could not withhold their tears.

James Joyce thought that becoming blind was the least important event in his life and Jorge Luis Borges does not find "a gradual summer twilight unbearable"; inner vision enabled him to dictate some of his finest writings during his long years of blindness. The blind poet sees the unseeable without being bewildered by earthly delusion.

The thought or threat of an illness often hurts as much as the affliction itself. It has recently been established that Emily Dickinson had a squint[66] and suffered from troubled eyesight, "a woe, the only one that ever made me tremble. It was the shutting out of all the dearest ones of time, the strongest friends of the soul−BOOKS." She was treated by a famous ophthalmologist in Boston, probably with an operation. She was naturally upset by the thought of becoming blind: "The medical man... might as well have said, 'Eyes be blind, heart be still'...",

39. E. Dickinson, In this daguerreo-type portrait of the poet, the difference in position of the light reflections in the pupils shows the deviation of her right eye. That was a trifle, enlarged in her poetical fantasy, compared to the squint of Dürer, who in this drawing of himself is warding off the confusing second image, seen by the divergent right eye.

the same cry of distress that Beethoven had uttered when threatened with deafness.

When one compares the manifestations of impaired sensory perception in artists, it seems that deafness, rather than blindness, has the greatest impact, particularly in view of the artist's special need for contact, except of course when decreased eyesight entirely prevents creation of visual art.[14] On closer consideration it is easy to appreciate that one gets more isolated in a deathly silent world, more excluded from human communion when one can no longer hear one's fellow-creatures and not participate in conversation. Goya, Swift and Beethoven are convincing examples.

The misanthropy and depression resulting from the sudden onset of deafness penetrate the art of Francisco Goya more obviously and more intensely than that of any other. Lighthearted in his youth, "the world's happiest being" in both word and art, spreading radiant light over the beautiful figures in his early painting, Goya was not spared the moments of melancholy that so often affect exalted spirits.[47] They were, however, light summer skies compared to the heavy thunderclouds to come. At the age of 47 he contracted a rare disease which left him blind for a short time and stone deaf forever.

Benumbed by his ill luck, Goya was at first quite incapable of engaging in any activity whatever, and when he eventually did resume painting his subject changed from pleasant dream to ghastly nightmare where he gave vent to the deepest despair and mistrust in all things human, as we see in, for example, the macabre "black pictures", painted during fits of melancholy in his later years.

In between he could, however, work in a lighter vein, and his misanthropic state of mind is less dominant in the pictures he painted on commission. Compare for instance the parts that he assigns to Time as a symbol. The colour scale in a large decoration, *Allegory on the adoption of the*

40. *F. Goya, In the allegory on the adoption of the constitution, Time is represented as an amiable old man who turns the hourglass to indicate the beginning of a new, happy era.*

constitution, is light and festive.[53] Time is represented as an amiable old man who does not let the hourglass run empty, but turns it to indicate the beginning of a new and hopefully happy era (Fig. 40). This is quite the opposite of some black paintings Goya kept for himself. In a letter to a friend he writes: "to engage my imagination which had been almost deadened by constant brooding over my sufferings, ... I have ventured upon a few ... pictures. In these paintings I have been able to find room for observations that would not fit easily into work made on order, and I also could give way to my fancy and inventive

41. *F. Goya, In the "black painting" of Saturn, Time is represented as a giant, devouring his own children, the hours, a drastic reminder of the sad fact that human time is temporary and that our moment of consciousness in the endless universe is not counted in giant figures.*

powers." Consider the picture of the giant, Saturn, eating his own children, which Goya hung in his dining room (Fig. 41). True, it is again Time, now indefatigable, creating hours, but also insatiable, devouring and extinguishing them just as rapidly, thereby rendering everything meaningless. This is akin to the opinion of a modern physicist:[68] "the more the universe seems comprehensible, the more it also seems pointless".

How Goya reminds one of Jonathan Swift! Menière's syndrome, with increasing dizziness and deafness, was an important contributory cause of Swift's deep mistrust of all humanity, which had the most extreme manifestations, such as his "Modest Proposal" that starving Irish children be fattened and exported to England for food!

Hearing is of prime importance for the artists who create with sounds, the composers. Beethoven started to lose his hearing in his twenties and spent his last years stone deaf in that most lonely of lonely states. He found this almost unbearable, as witness the moving words in the "Heiligen-Städter Testament":

"O you men, who think or say that I am malevolent, stubborn or misanthropic, how greatly do you wrong me—you do not know the secret reason for my behaviour—consider that for six years I have been suffering from an incurable condition . . .

I am deaf—oh, how would it be possible to admit the deficiency of a sense that I ought to possess to a more perfect degree than anybody else . . . I must live like an outcast; when I approach a gathering I become fearful of revealing my condition . . .

What a dejection when somebody next to me heard a flute and I did not hear anything, or when somebody heard the shepherd singing and I could not hear even that—such incidents made me desperate, I was not far from putting an end to my life. It was only Art, my art that restrained me—oh, I felt unable to leave this world before I had created what I felt had been assigned to me; and so I endured this miserable life—really miserable.

Patience must be my guide from now on. I have resolved, for good, I hope, to endure until the unyielding Parcae decide to break the thread ... To be forced to become a Philosopher at the age of 28 is not easy—and least of all for an artist."

Beethoven was, however, not always guided by patience. In the *Sonata appassionata* he bares his soul and gives free rein to despair and a heaven-storming defiance of his lamentable infirmity. But on the whole he succeeded better in becoming a Philosopher than his companions in misery, the unrestrained court-painter in Madrid and the venomous Dean from Dublin. For instance, it was under these circumstances that Beethoven composed the *Pastoral Symphony*, so elevated above human misery and distress; indeed perhaps he attained these heights by a superhuman effort to endure his disability. It is pathetic to hear him rejoice in rendering the enchanting sounds of animated nature which he could now only hear in memory while his ears were buzzing, day and night.

An ear specialist has made the interesting experiment of manipulating tapes of Beethoven's music from this period so that we may hear how it sounded to Beethoven with his limited auditory reception. It is enlightening but not explanatory, and it remains an open, but certainly intriguing question whether Beethoven's compositions were influenced by his impaired hearing. Did this help to free him from convention and tradition, thereby permitting the development of radically new creations? Hector Berlioz, who never learned to play an instrument correctly except the drums, might give us a clue.[7] "When I consider the appalling number of miserable platitudes to which the piano has given birth which would never have seen the light had their authors been limited to pen and paper, I feel grateful to the happy chance that forced me to compose freely and in silence, and this has delivered me from the tyranny of the fingers, so dangerous to thought, and from the fascination which ordinary sonorities always exercise on a composer, to a greater or lesser degree."

In his later years, Beethoven was certainly delivered from "ordinary sonorities" and could only perceive his compositions with his "inner ear", the inaudible music that Keats describes in *Ode to a Grecian Urn:*

> Heard melodies are sweet, but those unheard
> Are sweeter; therefore, ye soft pipes, play on;
> Not to the sensual ear, but, more endear'd
> Pipe to the spirit ditties of no tone.

We will never know with certainty what the cause was for Beethoven's deafness, but some disputed signs indicate that he had Paget's disease. Beethoven's ear symptoms are precisely those found in many cases of this bone disease and he also demonstrated other characteristics. His skull grew to an impressive size, with an Olympian forehead, massive jaws and a protruding chin. Rossini describes how his eyes shone from underneath the thick eye-brows, as from the bottom of a cave. These features are evident in portraits of Beethoven in later years. One of those, drawn four years before Beethoven's death (Fig. 42), might well illustrate an anecdote told by Bettina Brentano. Beethoven was taking a walk with his friend Goethe when they met the imperial family. The poet politely stepped aside, lifting his hat, while the headstrong composer pushed his outgrown one firmer on the head and walked straight on.

As a composer, Smetana could actually describe the very sound, the buzzing in the ears, which was the first sign of the hearing disease that eventually left him deaf. In the last movement of his quartet, *Aus meinem Leben*, there is a sudden shrill tone depicting this ringing sound, the "tinnitus" which brings on the composer's despair over his approaching disability. The movement then ends in resignation to his unavoidable fate.

It is hard to imagine a more cruel game that disease has played with an artist than Gabriel Fauré's ear complaint. Not only did his hearing diminish but even the quality of tone changed so that he heard out of tune, perceiving treble tones one third above and bass tones one third below the right note. He never heard his late compositions the way he had conceived them; "I only hear horrors", the ageing master lamented[22].

42. J. P. Lyser, a drawing of Beethoven, four years before his death, demonstrates typical signs of Paget's disease with large head and prominent forehead.

Agonizing pain. Two poets and one painter with gallstones

Intense pain, one of the most powerful sensations of life, has been vividly described by many artists and authors. Probably from personal experience, Shakespeare found that:

> There was never yet philosopher
> That could endure the toothache patiently
> However they have writ the style of gods
> and made a push of chance and sufferance.

Milton agreed:

> "But pain is perfect misery, the worst
> Of evils, and, excessive, overturns
> All patience".

The two could not foresee the spiritual strength of Immanuel Kant. This philosopher was an ascetic health pedant with strict rules, such as always to breathe through the nose, not through the mouth, to avoid catching common colds. He stressed the importance of a fixed timetable for eating and sleeping and always stopped thinking of complicated and exciting matters well ahead of bedtime. We can therefore understand his distress when his sleep was disturbed by disease – agonizing attacks of gout that turned his toes a glowing red.

In a stoic attempt to distract his mind from the pain, he forced himself to concentrate on some indifferent, trivial

43. A. Böcklin, Agony of pain in realistic form. The Swiss master was annoyed with an unappreciative art committee. He revenged himself on the six members by sculpting their portraits in caricature. He must have been particularly mad at this one.

matter (but no sheep-counting for a learned philosopher; the "trivial" subject he chose was the associations conjured up by the name *Cicero!*). This mitigated the pain, he fell asleep and was henceforth convinced that even severe pain can be controlled by willpower alone in most patients (apart from women and children, whom Kant, a bachelor and a son of his age, pronounced devoid of such power). He concluded that "It is unbelievable what a human being, even while suffering, can achieve through strong willpower – suffering might, in fact, by the only means of attaining that height of willpower".[31]

Karen Blixen, author of *Seven Gothic Tales*, showed convincingly that strong willpower is not a male privilege. Her husband gave her good reasons for jealousy but poor consolation when he also infected her with syphilis which was to cause her terrible agonies. She declared that "all sorrows can be borne if you put them into a story".

If Thomas De Quincey had been as stoic as Kant and Karen Blixen and not surrendered to his trigeminal neuralgia, he would probably not have become a drug addict and we would have missed the most initiated and eloquent narration there is of the effect of both the use and the abuse of opium. His abhorrence of toothache is expressive: "Two things blunt the general sense of horror which would else connect itself with toothache – viz., first, its enormous diffusion; hardly a household in Europe being clear of it, each in turn having some one chamber intermittently echoing the groans extorted by this cruel torture. A second cause is found in its immunity from danger – supposing toothache liable in ever so small a proportion of its cases to a fatal issue, it would be generally ranked as the most dreadful amongst human maladies."

Abdominal colic is often a symptom of more serious illness. In the 1820s two poets in different parts of Europe suffered badly from gallstone disease – Walter Scott[50] and

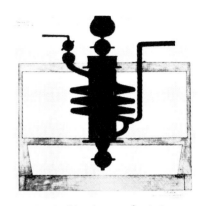

44. *F. Picabia, Agony of pain in symbolic form. His Paroxysm of Pain is actually grinding.*

45. *H. Matisse, Agony of pain in innate form.*

Esaias Tegnér. They exemplify how the same disease may have entirely different effects on different personalities. Their case histories were remarkably similar from a medical viewpoint—but what a disparity in reaction and responce between the robust Scotsman and the sensitive Swede!

Walter Scott was not overly concerned. During the attacks he roared like a bull, so that people could hear him on the road outside Abbottsford, and one night, feeling that he was dying, he bade farewell to his children; but as soon as the pain ceased he forgot his suffering.

Tegnér, on the other hand, was deeply disturbed and although witty as always, anticipated an untimely death: "New Year's Eve I got a Colic which I thought was going to bring both my poetical and theological life to a close and thereby teach me a variety of things about which both Poetics and Symbolics have left me in some uncertainty . . . I know that we all must die. Nevertheless, under the circumstances it would be somewhat inconvenient, if not for me, at least for my family. However, only a fool complains about the inevitable. Resignation is the sum of life's wisdom and the slightest consideration should teach us to make the best of the bad bargain which we call life—a bargain which we are sure to lose anyway."

Both patients learned that even friends in need can be a nuisance; in Scott's case, the Earl of Buchan called with the Christian wish of relieving Scott's mind about the arrangements for his funeral, all of which he could safely leave in the Earl's hands! Tegnér had a friend who wrote, "Thank heavens you are well again. The news of this illness scared me terribly for good reasons: in this year alone I have lost three friends from my early days." No wonder the addressees became discouraged!

The two poets reacted quite differently to the general effect of the disease. Scott bore up courageously and wrote, "I should be a great fool, and a most ungrateful wretch to complain of such inflictions as these. My life has been, in all its private and public relations, as fortunate perhaps as was ever lived, up to this period; and whether pain or misfortune may lie behind the dark curtain of futurity, I am already a sufficient debtor to the bounty of Providence to be resigned to it."

Poor Tegnér was more pathetic: "I can no longer hope for health or happiness: instead I hope that God will, until the end, provide me with the strength of mind, which in our sub-lunary world so often has to substitute for Providence. If my little personage must return whence it came, to drown in the large fountainhead or float around for some time like a bubble, reflecting the sky and a strange light; whether this occurs some months sooner or later seems to be of ever diminishing importance."

The disease thus added vital elements to the two authors' experience, bringing suffering to their lives but valuable material for their work.

Their literary activity was influenced in different degrees. Scott, with "the strength of a team of horses", continued to write during his attacks, but probably feared that the quality of his fiction suffered, because when he subsequently read what he had written in this condition he could not recollect a single incident, character or conversation: "When I was so dreadfully ill that I could hardly speak five minutes without loss of breath, I found that the exertion of dictating the nonsense . . . suspended for a time the sense of my situation."

Even if Scott himself could not recollect any of the incidents that he had invented while suffering, even if he thought that he had dictated nonsense during his illness, it is hard for us, his readers, to agree—on the contrary, *Ivanhoe*, though written mostly between bodily convulsions, became one of his most popular romances; a beautiful demonstration of mind's triumph over matter.

The influence of the illness on writing was much more

profound in Tegnér's case. His main project, *Fritiof's Saga*, had to be put aside for a while. He began using medical metaphors from his personal experience: "Even in my better, healthier days did I form Epigrams, but in a happy, light spirit. They were considered as harmless as they were meant to be, but now they are hardened, petrified bile and therefore hurting."

The disease was not the least important of the circumstances that caused a change in style and character of his poetry. Tegnér became disillusioned, often cynical, sometimes even desperate. One of his most personal poems, *The Spleen*, bears witness. It was written at a time when Tegnér was tortured by recurrent attacks of pain and fever from stones in the inflamed bile ducts:

I reached the summit of my life
Where waters separate and run
With frothy waves in different directions
It was clear up there, and wonderful to stand
I saw the Earth, t'was green and wondrous
And God was good and man was honest
Then, suddenly, a black, splenetic demon rose
And sank his teeth into my heart.
And see, at once the Earth was empty and forsaken
And sun and stars went dark in haste

— — —

A smell of corpses runs through life
The air of spring and summer's glory poisoned

— — —

My pulse beats fast as in my youthful days
But cannot count the times of agony
How long, how endless is each heartbeat's pain
O my tormented, burnt-out heart!
My heart? There is no heart within my breast
An urn there is, with ash of life enclosed.

The two authors also provide good examples of different attitudes to medical treatment. Scott professes early a high opinion of doctors and their work. In his novel *Surgeon's Daughter* he draws on his own knowledge when he describes the hardships of a Scottish country practitioner. In spite of them his doctor is devoted to his profession and has no desire to trade his practice for a comfortable city position. Scott has come to realize – and he does not change his view after being treated for his illness – that humanity is the physician's greatest virtue.[38]

Tegnér was dubious and sarcastic. A friend of his had fallen ill but was dissatisfied with the treatment he was receiving. His doctor had previously sent him some poems, adding that he wrote prescriptions better than poetry. This the friend had believed without difficulty but now, he said, he feared that the doctor had been unfair to his own poetry – a well-worded suspicion in Tegnér's opinion.

A century after the two poets, a great French painter was racked by the same kind of torments.[2] As Henri Matisse obstinately refused to be operated for his gallstones he suffered as much and as long as his brothers in misfortune. It was, in fact, the third serious disease that had a profound influence on this master's life and work – first the appendicitis of his youth, and then, in his seventies, cancer of the colon (see page 22), which was followed soon after by this latest problem.

For more than a year he had frequent attacks of severe pain, fever and jaundice. He was, however, more stoic than even Walter Scott; his proud nature did not permit him to complain – only his intimates knew about his agonies: "For my part, I spend most of my time in bed. I get up for an hour but, as I am not used to it, I am not very comfortable and it is with pleasure that I return to bed. I work regularly though, and paint in the afternoon." Thus, his strong character helped him to continue creating serene masterpieces, "the calm and mighty expressions of conquered pain". Only in the illustrations for *Pasiphae* does he let us divine his ordeal. In *L'Angoisse qui s'amasse* (Increasing anguish), the agony of pain itself wields the etching-needle with fine-spun subtlety (Fig. 45).

The story of the disease of Matisse also illustrates the disadvantage of consulting several doctors, each with his own opinion: "My dear Louis Aragon, I won't go to Switzerland this summer: I am too busy with the disease and the doctors; I have two teams – 1. One wants me to be operated – 2. The other not. The one that advises against is presided by a surgeon – my surgeon from Lyon, who knows the risks that I have been exposed to before and who does not want to subject me to them again."

One evening, the medical consultations turned into a riot and through the closed doors even the patient could hear the furious voice of Professor W. shouting that the heart of the patient would not stand an operation. No wonder that Matisse proclaims: "I have some right to defend my own skin. I have no character; I like to have an attack of pain now and then and prefer evading an operation – I could not endure it." It was probably under pressure of the different opinions that he quotes an old adage: "Listening to them, one would think that all doctors are assassins – excuse me!" He might as well have quoted Ben Jonson who, three centuries earlier, likewise had been ill and dissatisfied with the medical treatment. He expressed his angry feelings *To Dr Empirick:*

> When men a dangerous disease did scape
> Of old, they gave a cock to Aesculape.
> Let me give two, that doubly am got free
> From my disease's danger, and from thee.

Digression: artists' opinions of medicine and doctors

The irony of Matisse, the sarcasm of Jonson are echoes of numerous complaints about doctors through the ages. For the early ones, at least, there were good reasons. The treatment of Scott and Tegnér reminds us that they lived in an era when medicine had not yet entered the Age of Enlightenment and still retained many mediaeval errors. Disease was thought to be caused by some vitiated and impure matter in the blood, which had to be diverted. This idea lay behind the extensive use of bleedings, blisterings, emetics and catharsis. During one year, Louis XIII was prescribed 47 bleedings, 212 purges and 215 enemas! The king had to pay dearly for the special attention as he died young.

Lord Byron's life was also shortened by excessive bloodlettings even though he defended himself irascibly. When his doctors insisted, he became utterly disgusted and expressed his conviction that more people have died from doctor's lancets than from soldiers' lances. For centuries, men of light and learning expressed similar doubts about doctors' capacities, jokingly, sarcastically or bitterly, according to the degree of their disappointment. To Voltaire, the worst scourges of humanity are war, theologians and doctors. Montaigne[27] and Molière[9] were other sharp critics. Both suffered lingering disease and appreciated the value of health; the former says that "Health is a precious thing . . . without it our life becomes painful and offensive; pleasure, wisdom, science and virtue tarnish and fade away." The wise and sensible essayist was an adherent of stoicism: "We have to endure patiently the rules of our predicament: we are going to age, to grow weak and to get ill, in spite of all medicine."

He had more confidence in the healing power of nature than in that of drugs, and he despised doctors – doubting not only their ability, but also their honour: "They have more consideration for their own reputation, and, consequently, for their profits, than for their patients' interest." He goes as far as to suggest that some doctors do not hesitate to impair the condition of their patients in order to earn more, and summarizes his opinion, "I have always despised medicine but when I get ill, I don't conform to it – instead I get to hating and fearing it and I ask those who urge me to take medicaments at least to wait until I have regained strength and health to enable me to stand the effort and the risk of taking them."

The bitter joke that one needs good health to endure medical treatment was appropriated by Molière, one of the fiercest adversaries of medicine, when he says about himself in *Le Malade imaginaire* that he was not strong enough to stand the remedies, it was all he could do to bear the disease itself. This is not the last time we meet such sarcasms – disappointment with medical treatment of incurable disease is, alas, still with us. The prescription of potent drugs can be like trying to exorcise the Devil with Beelzebub. The dying Flannery O'Connor was forced to realize that "the medicine and the disease run neck and neck to kill you".

When Molière deals with doctors, there is not a trace of his usual joviality – only the harshest mockery. "Why does he need four doctors – is not one enough to kill a patient?"

His rancour was well founded:

> Your best knowledge is pure nonsense,
> Vain and imprudent doctors,
> With your fine Latin words you cannot cure
> The suffering, that is driving me to despair.

The suffering that exasperated Molière, the disease that he tried to bear, was tuberculosis. While his physicians proposed treatment that could only weaken him further, his health gradually failed. The consumptive cough and the shortness of breath made stage performance increasingly difficult. As a born comedian, he exploited his symptoms in his acting, passing them off as intentional comic turns and making the effect as irresistible as the coughing attack.

At the close of the fourth performance of *Le Malade imaginaire*, when Molière played the part of Argan, he was overtaken by profuse blood spitting and the curtain fell as rapidly on the play as on the life of the actor who

46. A. Watteau, "The confounded assassins", members of the Medical Faculty examine the blood they have drawn from the painter and attack him with their enema syringes.

could no longer make believe. Behind the bursts of laughter after this comedy[3] we will always discern the faint sound of a sob.

Antoine Watteau also died young from tuberculosis. He shared in painting the same low opinion of medicine that Montaigne and Molière expressed in words: their doctors appear, drawn to life in one of his paintings (Fig. 46). He depicts himself already at the cemetery, wrapped in his dressing gown, trying to escape his tormentors, the Medical Faculty who attack him with their enema syringes. The very thought of death is with him, barely concealed by his usual graceful fancy, but with a shrill tinge bordering on the grotesque. Only in the inscription does the cry of distress, pain and agony break from his lips without restraint: "What have I done, confounded assassins, to so incur your wrath?" In order to enjoy fully the scenes described by Molière and depicted by Watteau we may add an accompaniment by Rossini as he in tones ridicules Doctor Bartolo, the basso-buffoon in *The Barber of Seville*.

Through the chorus of excited voices condemning the medical profession we may discern a soft note of appreciation played by the composer Marin Marais (1656–1728). After foresightedly having written his will, Marais evidently underwent an operation for stone in the bladder —at any rate he wrote a beautiful piece for viola entitled *Description of the Cystotomy*, one of the earliest examples of instrumental program music. He sounds still agitated when describing with rapid notes the sequences of the painful and dangerous procedure, which in those days was so dramatic that tickets were sold to those who wanted to watch the horror.

Two strong servants held the legs of the victim (Fig. 47) while a third one sat astride on his chest, holding up the scrotum. The "surgeon" introduced a metallic catheter through the urinary duct into the bladder and then made a rapid incision toward its tip through the perineum. When

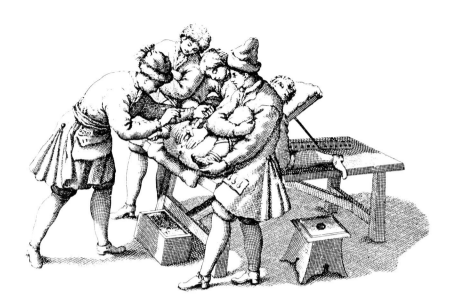

the bladder was opened, the stone was delivered with a
forceps. The mortality rate of the procedure was 60%.

These are the headings of the composition: "The view
of the operating table—trembling at the sight of it—the
decision to mount—in position—folding of the table—
serious thoughts—tying the legs up to the arms—the
incision—introduction of the forceps—here the stone is
delivered—here one nearly loses one's breath—blood is
flowing—here the legs are released—here one is put back
to bed." No wonder the composer, after such an ordeal,
needed no less than three gay dances—entitled "churching
of a woman after childbirth"!—to fully express the extent
of his relief and the pleasure of recovery (see page 125).

Even Goya, in the nineteenth century, had good reason
to feel contempt for his doctors, whom he represents as
donkeys sitting at their patient's bedside. Ultimately, medicine developed into science and in his old age
Goya found it fair to inscribe a double portrait of himself
and his doctor (Fig. 49) as follows, "Goya, in gratitude to
his friend Arrieta, whose skill and care saved his life dur-

*47. Anonymous, An illustration of
the operation for stone in the bladder
in the eighteenth century.*

48. F. Goya, The disappointed painter saw the doctor as a donkey at the bedside.

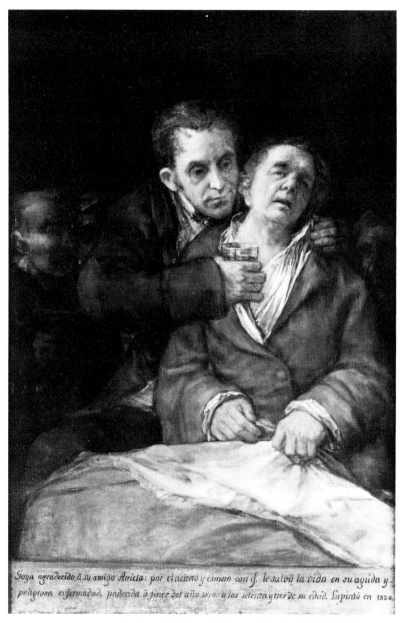

Goya agradecido, à su amigo Arrieta: por el acierto y esmero con q. le salvó la vida en su aguda y peligrosa enfermedad, padecida à fines del año 1819. à los setenta y tres de su edad. Lo pintó en 1820.

49. F. Goya, Many years later he changed his mind and expressed gratitude to the doctor who saved his life.

ing the severe and dangerous illness from which he suffered at the age of seventy-three." In this picture, the ageing master, by virtue of his art, gives individual and lasting presence to the brief moments that precede extinction.

One of the last, but by no means the least rancorous of doctor-haters was George Bernard Shaw. The background is that he became ill with caries of a leg. This generally is a lingering disease, especially when, as in Shaw's case, fragments of dead bone are formed which often have to await nature's expulsion. In severe cases even amputation might be considered. Shaw's patience was limited and he became sick to death, or rather furious with his doctor:

"The tragedy of illness at present is that it delivers you helplessly into the hands of a profession which you deeply mistrust." He gave free rein to his scorn and disgust in *The Doctor's Dilemma*. It was above all the fact that doctors have a pecuniary interest in the patient's disease that upset him. In the preface to the play he argues: "I cannot knock my shins severely without forcing on some surgeon the difficult question: 'Could I not make a better use of a pocketful of guineas than this man is making of his leg? Could he not write as well – or even better – on one leg than on two? ... artificial legs are now so well made that they are really better than natural ones." It is hard to tell whether Shaw would have written better on one leg – but it certainly would have set fire to him! The rage once expressed by Montaigne and later by Molière rings again in his observation that "It is simply unscientific to allege or believe that doctors do not under existing circumstances perform unnecessary operations and manufacture and prolong lucrative diseases."

Shaw's severe criticism of the "existing circumstances" that doctors had an economic interest in the patient's illness led to early steps towards socialized medicine in Great Britain.

Tuberculosis

In the history of creative work, there are many who, like Watteau and Molière, had their work influenced and their lives shortened by tuberculosis. One has the impression that this disease often exerted a singular effect on their talent. The slight fever livened the associations and filled the imagination with fantastic, dreamlike pictures. A greater zest for life, which could not be satisfied in reality because of the lassitude produced by the disease, finds an outlet instead in the realm of fantasy. In Watteau's later paintings, in particular, we find these pathetic, impassioned attempts to keep hold of fleeting joy during lessons of love and to remain on Cythera—the island where no worries or suffering exist.

In *The Lesson of Love* the lone musician is playing to a pretty girl who is turning away from him. Carl Nordenfalk[46] suggests that this guitar-player is a "symbolic self-portrait, the melancholic consumptive to whom it was never given to drain the cup of life's pleasure, which he so brimmingly offers us in his art" (Fig. 50).

In *Pilgrimage to Cythera*, Kenneth Clark[16] sees the resemblance to the ailing Mozart, probably suffering from progressive uremia, who was well aware of the ephemeral character of human pleasures: "The delicate relationship between these men and women who have spent a few hours on the Island of Venus and must now return reminds one of the rapturous stirrings that precede the departure of the confident lovers in *Così fan tutte*."

We find the same feeling of sweet sadness in the poetry of Keats and in Chopin's *Nocturnes*—these tenderly

50. *A. Watteau, In "The Lesson of Love", the guitar player might be a symbolic self portrait, a melancholic consumptive.*

melancholic feverdreams. Both suffered from consumption and the poor, deserted Chopin worked himself to death during the last stages of disease. He was then in London, the same place to which Carl Maria von Weber once had traveled, feverish, suffocating and spitting blood to attend the first night of his opera, *Oberon*, and, shortly thereafter, the last night of his life. In the *Funeral Sonata*,

Chopin expresses the agony that seized him on leaving Valdemosa monastery after his last sojourn with George Sand. The famous Funeral March is interrupted for a few moments by a nostalgic remembrance of happier days but soon succeeded by a presto that has been compared to the flutter of the night breeze amongst tombstones – the concert where no encores are granted.

John Keats had a medical education and was aware of his fate after nursing his brother, who died young from tuberculosis. Describing the ominous event of his own disease, a profuse hemorrhage of the lungs, he writes to his fiancée[62]: "On the night I was taken ill – when so violent a rush of blood came to my lung that I felt nearly suffocated – I assure you I felt it possible I might not survive, and at that moment thought of nothing but you."

He sees the progress of his disease and the nature of his expectorations with the eyes of a doctor: "I know the color of that blood – it is arterial blood – I cannot be deceived in that color; that drop is my death warrant. I must die."

He tries to calm Fanny, his "dearest girl", by using moderation in speech; "this is unfortunate" and, as all humans, he at least makes an effort to deceive even himself, probably kindly supported by the euphoria which characterizes his disease: " 'Tis true that since the first two or three days other subjects have entered my head. I shall be looking forward to Health and the Spring and a regular routine of our old walks."

In his last years, consumed by a hopeless passion and wasted by disease, inappropriately treated, he reflects on the relations between disease and creation: "How astonishing does the chance of leaving the world impress a sense of its natural beauties on us."

Ode to a Nightingale, a love song to the ecstasy and eternal joy of life, is imbued with a conflicting longing for death as he had seen it in his brother:

Fade far away, dissolve, and quite forget
What thou among the leaves hast never known,
The weariness, the fever, and the fret
— — —

Where youth grows pale, and spectre thin, and dies;
Where but to think is to be full of sorrow
And leaden eyed despairs,
— —

Already with thee! tender is the night
And haply the Queen-Moon is on her throne,
— — —

Now more than ever seems it rich to die,
To cease upon the midnight with no pain,
While thou art pouring forth thy soul abroad
In such an ecstasy!
— — —

Thou wast not born for death, immortal Bird!

(Because his song remains the same through the centuries):

Perhaps the self-same song that found a path
Through the sad heart of Ruth, when sick for home,
She stood in tears amid the alien corn.

Man is born for death, since our songs are unique and our personality dies with us.

During the 19th century tuberculosis continued to reap a terrible harvest among youth and many promising artistic careers were cruelly severed. After the Keats brothers there were the Brontë sisters. Fatal disease and bouts of depression combine with poverty and a lonely life among the barren moors to form the gloomy background of their melodramatic fiction, which so well reflected contemporary, sentimental taste. Since the two oldest girls had died in childhood from galloping consumption, it was left to

51. C. Brontë, The writer has drawn a delicate portrait of her mild and submissive consumptive sister Anne.

the third, Charlotte, to bring up and soon also to nurse the two youngest. They differed a great deal from one another. Emily, who was able to complete *Wuthering Heights*, a solitaire of strange and singular lustre, before she succumbed to the disease, was withdrawn and headstrong, a lonely wanderer on the moors, whereas the youngest, Anne, who wrote ethereal verse like the *Psalm of Resignation* (page 20) was mild and submissive.

This difference also characterizes their reaction to the disease. The proud Emily sought solitude like a wounded animal and was reluctant to receive either care or compassion, while Anne thankfully accepted both.

Seeing her sisters die, Charlotte became intimately and tragically acquainted with the symptoms of progressing pulmonary tuberculosis; her descriptions in the chapter *The Valley of the Shadow of Death* are more vivid than those of any doctor. There is the ominous loss of appetite: "palatable food was as ashes and sawdust to her", replaced by increasing thirst. "She felt her brain in strange activity: her spirits were raised; hundreds of busy and broken, but brilliant thoughts engaged her mind.—The sick girl wasted like any snowwreath in thaw; she faded like any flower in drought". The helpless doctors are ridiculed: "One came, but that one was an oracle: he delivered a dark saying of which the future was to solve the mystery, wrote some prescriptions, gave some directions—the whole with an air of crushing authority—pocketed his fee, and went. Probably, he knew well enough he could do no good; but didn't like to say so." But Charlotte knew, "one alone reflected how liable is the undermined structure to sink in sudden ruin". The exhausted patient herself is torn between feelings of satiety with life and agony of death: "she usually buried her face deep in the pillow, and drew the coverlets close round her, as if to shut out the world and sun, of which she was tired; more than once, as she thus lay, a slight convulsion shook the sickbed, and a faint sob broke the silence round it. 'God grant me a little comfort before I die!' was her humble petition, 'sustain me through the ordeal I dread and must undergo!'"

Feverish dreams and failing strength announce the end. "Oh! I have had a suffering night. This morning I am worse. I have tried to rise. I cannot. Dreams I am unused to have troubled me." The desperately helpless nurse-sister prays humbly but demandingly, "with that soundless voice the soul utters when its appeal is to the Invisible:

'Spare my beloved,—Rend not from me what long affection entwines with my whole nature". She recognizes with horror the symptoms that announce the final extinction and resigns: "the watcher approaches the patient's pillow, and sees a new and strange moulding of the familiar features, feels at once that the insufferable moment draws nigh—and subdues his soul to the sentence he cannot avert, and scarce can bear!"

At the end of her difficult life Charlotte did indeed experience perfect but brief happiness in a late marriage. But in keeping with her misfortunes the token of her happiness—her pregnancy—proved fatal, the "nausea gravidarum", the vomiting and other strains caused her tuberculosis to flare up and end her life.

In his autobiographical *Ordered South*,[58] Robert Louis Stevenson describes the stages whereby the tubercular is "tenderly weaned from the passion of life".

Two Northern poetesses who died young exemplify how the disease first produces an intense zest for life and then

52. Harriet Löwenhjelm is touchingly lonely and forsaken in her disease. Death is waiting for the artist, ill at a sanatorium.
    "Am I tired unto death, rather tired, very tired, ill, and sad, and tired."

gradual lassitude (Fig. 52). Edith Södergran expresses an ecstatic and defiant feeling for life:

> We should love life's long hours of disease
> and narrow years of yearning
> as we love the short moments when the desert
> blossoms

Her later poetry is marked by cool resignation and a transcendental entering into the spirit of death:

> I long for the land that is not,
> For all things that are, I'm tired of desiring.

Like Keats, Anton Chekhov, another victim of tuberculosis, had a medical education: "Medicine is my lawful wife and literature my mistress." The parable indicates his real love and the "lawful wife" was soon deserted—but never forgotten: Medicine "significantly extended the area of my observations, enriched my knowledge, and only one who is himself a physician can understand the true value of this for me as a writer". Did it also, together with his disease, contribute to the resigned attitude which he shared with a whole series of indecisive or irresolute doctors in his fiction? "With me, a physician, there are also few illusions. Of course, I'm sorry for this—it somehow desiccates life." Chekhov developed his tuberculosis at an early age. As sometimes is the case with doctors, he stubbornly refused to accept his colleagues' diagnosis and carefully hid the telltale specks of blood on his handkerchief from the anxious eyes of his parents. Nevertheless, the secret preoccupation with his condition finds expression in many of his works, imbued with nostalgia and a melancholic foreboding of death, as in the closing lines of *The Black Monk*:

"Blood began to flow from his throat straight on to his breast.—He fell to the floor and called: 'Tania!' He called Tania, he called to the great gardens with their lovely flowers sprinkled with dew, he called to the park, to the pines with their rugged roots, to the fields of rye, to his wonderful science, to his youth, courage, joy, he called to life that was so beautiful. He saw on the floor, close to his face, a large pool of blood, and from weakness he could not utter another word, but an inexpressible, a boundless happiness filled his whole being."

Doctor Chekhov well knew and cherished the pre-terminal euphoria which makes our last departure easier by spreading a merciful veil over painful reality. Shostakovitch, who had spent long periods in a sanatorium, must have had a kindred feeling for his fellow-sufferer when he cited *The Black Monk* as the key to his 15th Symphony, having given death-agony as the key to his 14th.

D. H. Lawrence also tried to the very last to conceal his tuberculosis, from himself as well as from others, by giving it different names—flu, bronchitis, common cold. He transformed it into fiction by passing it on to Lady Chatterley's lover, the gamekeeper who was "curiously full of vitality, but a little frail and quenched"—not to the degree, however, that it prevented him from sharing the most violent physical ecstasies with the lady, herself ill and feeble from boredom and sexual starvation. The frank and detailed descriptions of their passion, trembling with excitement, shocked his contemporaries.

This new literary realism was coloured, even prompted, by Lawrence's illness. The novel was written during the last stages of his tuberculosis, when the toxins, circulating in his blood, made him weak and weary. Did his latent homosexual tendency facilitate his understanding of female sexuality?[48] Be that as it may, it is through Lady Chatterley that he expresses his lassitude—"Why don't I really care?"—and his fear of approaching death, of the "ghastly white tombstones—detestable as false teeth—which stick up on the hillside".

The disease also hampered Lawrence's own sexual

53. A. Beardsley, "As the dawn broke, Pierrot fell into his last sleep. Then upon tip-toe, silently up the stairs, came the comedians Arlecchina, Pantaleone, il Dottore and Columbina who with much love carried away upon their shoulders the white frocked clown of Bergamo, whither we know not".

activity; in fact, he became impotent. As so often occurs, the unsatisfied desire nourished erotic fantasies which in their feverish intensity resemble the dreams of puberty in which there is no end to the flowers, threaded in the pubic hair, "forget-me-not flowers in the fine brown fleece of the mound of Venus" and "a bit of creeping-jenny round his penis", not to mention other assorted localities.

All this gives *Lady Chatterley's Lover* the character of a consumptive novel. It has traits in common with the works of Aubrey Beardsley, who also gave vent to a restrained sexuality but in a more sophisticated form. With intricate artistry, this master drawer gave expression to the "fin de siècle" atmosphere and to "art nouveau". Tubercular since his boyhood, Beardsley was greatly affected by his disease and was well aware of his destiny: "yesterday I was laid out like a corpse with a haemorrhage. For me and my lung there seems to be little hope". – "I shall not live longer than did Keats" he said

54. A. Beardsley, The artist tied to Priapus, symbol of sexuality.

LYSISTRATA.

55. A. Beardsley, Lysistrata, shielding her cointe while the penis is as adoringly decorated as that of Lady Chatterley's lover.

and drew himself lying in bed, dying, while his co-actors on the stage of life assembled to bid farewell (Fig. 53). Still he worked with the intensity of a condemned man — as he literally was.

In his refined, decadent art we find both sexual hunger

and defiance. Beardsley was haunted by feverish, erotic fantasies, arising from illness and from sexual repression and concealment. His friend Yeats tells that Beardsley's sexual desire under the pressure of disease had become insatiable and he admits this with a portrait of himself tied to Priapus (Fig. 54). Beardsley implies an illness-related impotence. He tries to satisfy his desire instead, and vindicates himself by making indecent drawings. With progressing disease and weakness his art became increasingly obscene[69]—but it also reached new heights of elegance, artistry and skill. The last sheets, illustrating *Lysistrata*, drawn between haemorrhages from the lung, defied publication for a long time, unfortunately, as there rarely has been created more charming and loveable, innocently candid, erotic art (Fig. 55).

A more playful but equally defensive attitude towards the disease was taken by the German poet Christian Morgenstern at the turn of the century. He caught tuberculosis from his mother and spent his short life in and out of sanatoria. He faced his illness and asserted his inner freedom with sick humor. In the spirit of François Villon he made fun of his tragic fate in grotesque *Gallows Songs*.[44] He observed that "From the gallow hill you see the world differently and you see different things than others do". We find them in his *Gallows Brother's Spring Song:*

> Spring, even on *our* splinter, springs;
> O sing for the blissful days!
> Here, now, in the breeze there swings,
> Now, over there, there sways
>
> A young stem yearning toward the light
> Out of a woodworm's bore.
> I feel almost as if I might
> Be what I am no more.

108

56. I. Arosenius, St. George and
the dragon — the artist fighting his
hemophilia, the bleeding disease
which finally killed him.

Miscellaneous physical illnesses

The Swedish painter of fairy-tales, Ivar Arosenius, died from hemophilia, the bleeding disease, when he was only 30.[10] This hereditary complaint had already claimed his elder brother, who at 14 bled to death after having a tooth extracted. Arosenius was deeply conscious of the constant danger that hung over him and he depicted it with bloody realism. Never has a dragon bled so convincingly and profusely as the one which had encountered the artist in the shape of Saint George (Fig. 56), fighting the disease. The haemorrhages were accompanied by much pain and restricted his movements; the slightest blow or bruise produced nasty effusions and painful swelling of the joints. These circumstances had a fundamental effect on his artistic work—both of a conducive and modifying nature. During the long periods when, as a child, he had to stay in bed, he amused himself by drawing and painting. He thus acquired a fantastic manual dexterity; few other artists have found it so easy to transfer their ideas to paper. Not only the form but also the content of his art was affected by the disease. From the outset it manifested itself mainly as a desperate revolt, a wild desire to forget his condition and to extract from life what it had to offer as quickly and as intensely as possible. He paints himself weak and exhausted, riding his pegasus to seek oblivion with the girl and the bottle (Fig. 57), and in some self-portraits the profusely bleeding heart represents a terrible reality, far from romantic convention.

Arosenius was rescued from the wear and tear of his bohemian life through a blissful marriage, which yielded

him some years of unalloyed happiness. His greatest joy is his little daughter, for whom he paints some of the most beautiful, imaginative, and eloquent fairy-tale illustrations to be found anywhere—for instance, that of the poor beggar-boy who does not join in the general hurry and scurry, and yet—or perhaps, just for that reason—finds the golden goose and accordingly gains the princess's hand and half the kingdom.

Arosenius's happiness was not unclouded, for the dangerous disease still lurked. Having once nearly died from a nosebleed, he worked with tremendous intensity, knowing that his days were numbered. At the jolliest feast Death suddenly takes a seat as an unbidden, fearsome guest, *A Macabre Company* (Fig. 59). Death was indeed near, and not only in Arosenius's imagination. While his wife was sleeping on New Year's Eve he sat working, even though he had a sore throat. Suddenly she awakened to find her husband choking. Before help could be called he was dead—from bleeding in the throat—and a life, beautiful but all too brief, had ended.

One of the most original artists of our time was Paul Klee. Highly talented and musical, he found new modes

57. I. Arosenius, The weak and exhausted artist on his Pegasus, consoled by girl and bottle.

58. I. Arosenius, Boy returning the golden goose requests his reward.

of expression for art which transmitted the spontaneous joy of the hand and mind in forming new pictures in new colours; intricate, previously unconceived constellations. He loved "to go for a walk with a line". His imagination was original and exuberantly rich. We see how much fun he must have had in constructing the peculiar and fantastic piece of architecture, which he calls *Sängerhalle* ("Hall of the Singers") (Fig. 60). It must have been a happy artist who wielded the pen and brush in this picture and hoisted the flag on the turret!

When he was only 40, however, Klee began to suffer from scleroderma, a most serious disease that involves shrinkage of the skin and underlying muscles. It is still incurable and usually leads to death in a matter of four or five years. It progresses inexorably and is also penetrative. Tragically, this progression is obvious to the patient; almost day by day he can see death approaching. Most of us are already undergoing, or will soon develop, the

59. *I. Arosenius, Death is macabre company at the jolliest feast, with the Swedish poet Bellman's words:*

Empty your glass for Death awaits you,
Pluck your guitar
Tune your strings and sing of the springtime of Life.

pathological changes that ultimately terminate life, but fortunately they are concealed from us; we cannot see our own degenerative process. This helps to conceal the briefness of life. But the complaint which destroyed Klee could not be concealed and it was not long before he found that it affected not only his mind but his art. He experienced difficulty in executing detailed pictures because of the rigidity of his joints. He illustrates his condition in a drawing of a sad figure, *Ein Gestalter* (a creator) holding a crayon in his crippled hand (Fig. 36)—a situation similar to that of Renoir (Fig. 35) and Dufy with their arthritic joints—but Klee's was hopeless.

His work now loses its gay, exhilarated character and thoughts of death and tranformation are his constant companions—nearly his only ones as he experienced the loneliness of most of us when approaching death and lived his last years in utter spiritual solitude;[26] "one dies alone", said Pascal. He expressed his agony only through

60. P. Klee, Hall of the singers. The artist was happy "to go for a walk with a line".

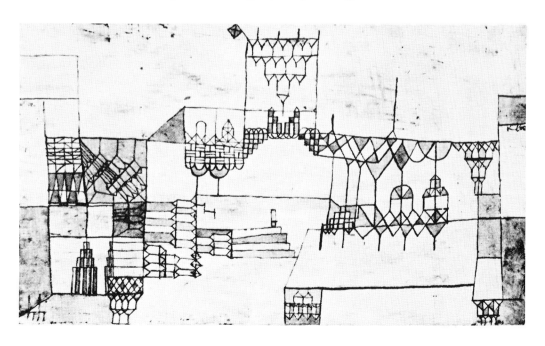

his work, "never have I drawn so much, nor so intensely" and he confessed: "I create—in order not to cry." His late drawings form a funereal suite of rare vehemence with titles like *will dabei sein* (prefers to remain) and *trennt sich schwer* (departs reluctantly). One of the last, *durchhalten!* (endure!) (Fig. 61a) is a moving expression of the artist's effort to keep up his courage in view of life's tragedy and to follow Montaigne's advice: "endure, suffer and keep quiet". The drawn lines around the mouth resemble the artist's own sad, strained features, marked by disease (Fig. 61b). It was not long before *The Sick one in the Boat* had Charon as oarsman (Fig. 62).

A Swedish poet was similarly afflicted with a horrible disease, progressive myasthenia or muscular debility, which causes increasing paralysis; this was Hjalmar Gull-

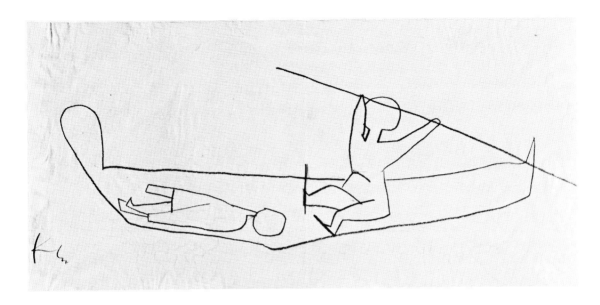

berg, whose harrowing words show that extreme human
misery, caused by severe bodily illness which can hardly
be tolerated, may still be expressed in beautiful and moving verse. In the form of a poem he replies to a young man
who complained to him about the mental distress which
arose from his own creative endeavours:

> But I am old
> and many are the letters of this kind
> that I have read.
> I am passing through a crisis.
> Maltreated flesh is real in a way
> different from a soul in distress.
> Proof of this I found
> in the stinking pus that flowed.
> Now I am reached by a fragrance of the bird-cherry.
> You are a young man in good health.

In his late poetry there are reflections of Gullberg's serious disease, noticeable also in his handwriting (Fig. 63).
He expresses a longing for annihilation, "one wish only,

115

only one—others have so many", and reveals a shocking and pathetic knowledge of the lamentable final decomposition of our physical being. His mouthpiece is the man "who found Ophelia, dead in the mire":

"I found Ophelia. She rose to the surface in the reeds, her hair undone. She was much changed . . .
Death through pouring water
is what I found in my nets: A swollen
mermaid put to fermentation by the brook.
What did I do first when I found, in all her finery,
a court lady in the wet mire?
I saw what I saw. Then I vomited in the reeds."

When Gullberg was threatened with a worsening of his disease – another flow of stinking pus – he chose to follow Ophelia into the wet mire.

Rainer Maria Rilke displayed the same heroic endurance during the disease, leukemia, that ended his life after several years of agony, and he is said to have refused analgesics. After he had outlined the first two *Duino elegies* he became poetically silent for several years and must have doubted whether he ever would complete them. Then, in a remarkable flare of inspiration, in a few weeks he completed the ten elegies and his ecstatic medi-

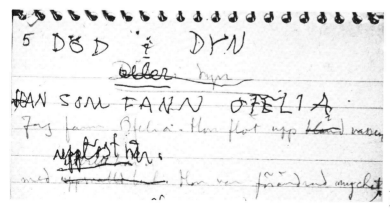

63. *Dead in the mire. Facsimile. The shaky corrections in his formerly neat hand and the tragically drastic subject testify to Hjalmar Gullberg's progressive muscle disease.*

tations on death and poetry, the *Sonnets to Orpheus*, "Everything in only a few days, it was an indescribable storm, a hurricane in my spirit". Shortly thereafter he showed the first signs of disease:

> "Come thou, the last one whom I own,
> The horrid pain in my malignant blood!"

Rilke was fond of flowers and found the height of rapture in the rose — he was actually rapt *in extremis*, pricked by a thorn when disease had deprived him of all defense against infection and death. His consolation, if any, was to have a rose named after him.

This notable coincidence of illness and creativity has prompted conjectures about a causal connection. An imaginative theory is that the spate of creativity was transformed psychosomatically into the disease, "everything that is fiber and tissue within me was strained to the breaking point". From a medical point of view, however, the most probable link (if any) is that the poet, consciously or unconsciously, felt the disease coming on and, with a presentiment of death, hurried to fulfill his mission before it was too late. This possibility is supported by Rilke himself: "But now it's *done*. Done. Done. *Amen*. So this is what I survived for, through everything. Through all of it. And that, after all, was what I needed. *Only* this".

Béla Bartók, who died with the same kind of "malignant blood", complained that he had "to go with so much still to say". Progressively emaciated and excited by continuous fever, he composed his swan-song, the third piano concerto. In the shadow of death, and pitifully exiled, he recalls the riches and possibilities of life in tunes which have their sources in the folk songs from the land of his fathers.

A female counterpart is the fatally ill but strongminded Flannery O'Connor,[49] who fought a natural self-pity with grim humour, and looked evil straight in the eye, in her life as well as in fiction, where "a good man is hard to find", and a nice girl is apt to get fooled, especially if she is lame. Her disease, *lupus erythematosus*, cripples by affecting the joints, but later attacks one organ after another. "My father had it—but at that time there was nothing for it but the undertaker; now it can be controlled with the ACTH"—and this gave her another invaluable fifteen years to live and work. In the English term, "butterfly rash", there is the same lighthearted, deceptive way of expressing a sinister reality that we find in her writing. "I have never been anywhere but sick. In a sense, sickness is a place, more instructive than a long trip to Europe, and it is always a place where there's no company, where nobody can follow."

She even plays on the word *lupus*, Latin for wolf, when the illness finally got the better of her: "the wolf, I am afraid, is inside, tearing up the place"—and she faltered with anemia and kidney insufficiency. "I had a blood transfusion Tuesday, so I am feeling sommut better and for the last two days I have worked one hour each day and my my I do like to work. I et up that one hour like it was filet mignon." In this misery she found that "what you have to measure out, you come to observe closer, or so I tell myself". Her close observations are related in a mature, uniquely personal style in her last stories, completed when she was dying. Her strong religious belief may have combined with the continuous threat of a fatal disease to engender her fascination with unrelenting fate as well as with merciless characters and doomed individuals.

At the end of our dance of death with poets, painters and composers, we will let Flannery O'Connor join hands with Juan Gris and Gustav Mahler.

Juan Gris was the third of the great cubists, somewhat younger than Picasso and Braque. He was their friend and

118

64. *J. Gris, Cubistic painting by the healthy artist.*

comrade, as well as their equal in artistic creativeness, becoming perhaps the most discerning. He often used a more vibrant colour scale than Picasso and Braque, especially in the early days of cubism, when these two artists excelled in subtle harmonies of greys and browns. Juan Gris was much taken by this new possibility of deriving new values from reality, by viewing a subject from several angles at once, as Cézanne had done, and unfolding it so as to produce intricate patterns, with overlapping angles and triangles (Fig. 64).

By nature Juan Gris was melancholic and withdrawn. During a period in the late twenties he felt that his work had become somewhat cold, a little too intellectual and, like others before him, he cherished an ambition to reach beyond himself. He wished to convey more human life and warmth, but to this end he violated his individuality in painting, and all are agreed that his work lost in artistic power and intensity. The paintings seem a little inflated, the colours drier and the high artistic merit of his earlier work is clearly absent. At this time Juan Gris had the first symptoms of a disease which in the course of a few years was to terminate his life. He had had scarlet fever and ultimately died from chronic renal failure. The diagnosis of uremia was not made at once; he had increasingly severe attacks of asthma which were erroneously considered to be of bronchial origin and for which injec-

65. *J. Gris, Painted while the artist was dying from uremia but regained his original artistic strength.*

tions, sedatives and a change of climate were prescribed. He found it difficult to work for long periods at a time and complained that some of his pictures took on a sickish tone. Still he continued to paint with great willpower. His last pictures show that his illness had induced him to abandon all ambitions to get outside himself – here he again gives full expression to his own strong personality and recovers his original greatness (Fig. 65).

Contemplating these last heroic efforts of Gris, Gustav Mahler's immensely beautiful and sad chords of *Das Lied von der Erde* ring in the background. The inevitability of death and the hope of resurrection had been a constant theme in this composer's art ever since a slight heart murmur had been discovered (see page 42). When the ominous streptococci settled on his heart valves after a throat infection, the disease took a fatal turn. Aware that death was imminent, Mahler composed in a more solemn and serene vein, a definite farewell to life.

He writes to Bruno Walter[41]: "You do not know what is going on within me; but it is certainly not the hypochondriac fear of death that you surmise. That I shall have to die, I had already realized.—But without trying to explain or describe something for which there are perhaps no words at all, I'll just tell you that at one blow I have simply lost all that I ever attained of clarity and equanimity; that I stood face-to-face with nothingness and now, at the end of life, am again a beginner who must find his feet". Theodor Reik,[45] the psychoanalyst, discusses Mahler's attitude: "One can trace through his letters, through certain things he said, but most of all through his music how his reaction to the near end was changing, how he himself changed, how he discarded everything that was alien to him. When he confronts perdition naked, there is no more sentimentality, no false emotionality, no false tones. Here a man rises highest at the moment he is crushed . . . There, where others sink, he soars to an unsurpassable height."

Epilogue

The song is born of sorrow
But out of song is gladness bred[60]

A salient feature of an artist's work has at times been
ascribed erroneously to a disease, as when the elongated
figures of El Greco were thought to be due to astigmatism, a visual defect. The numerous examples in the fore-
going pages have shown, however, that illness has,
indeed, often deeply influenced not only the life but also
the work of great authors, artists and composers. Hans
Christian Andersen of fairy-tale fame is emphatic about
the power of pain and its prominent place in the history of
culture. His *Aunt Toothache* is the strongest advocate:
"So you are a writer' she said, 'well I will write you up in
all the poetic measures of pain!' It was as if I had got a
glowing awl into the cheekbone! 'Do you admit now that
I am mightier than Poetry, Philosophy, Mathematics and
all of Music? Mightier than all these sensations depicted in
Painting and Sculpture?—and older also". A raging
attack suffices to convince the victim that suffering and
pain make a big difference (see Shaw and Updike, p. 17).
Many authors, artists and composers have themselves
been well aware of the important rôle that their disease
has played, as seen in the quotations from Proust (p. 43)
and Byron (p. 57).

This of course does not imply that suffering is a prere-
quisite for artistic creation, nor that a creator has to be ill in
order to make suffering real to us. Thomas Mann goes
through both tuberculosis and syphilis–but only in his
fiction. Hieronimus Bosch paints gruesome pictures of
terrible pain that he never experienced himself, and Johan
Sebastian Bach, though hale and hearty, enables us,

through vehement strains of music, to attend the summit of suffering, the flagellation of Christ.

The effect of a disease may be apparent in many ways. It is beyond dispute when it is the main reason why the artist dedicated himself to artistic creation, as when Matisse started painting when appendicitis interrupted his legal career, or when Vivaldi took up composing because asthma prevented him from conducting Mass.

When it comes to the direct influence of disease on the work, even the technical execution may be affected. This is apparent in the late paintings of the half-blind Monet, which suffer from coarse brushstrokes and a deranged sense of colour (see tailpiece). We learn from them that disease occasionally may influence the direction of art's development, independent of the creator's own intentions. With the confused design and strange colours in his later works, Monet unawares took a step from reality and thus inspired the transition towards abstract art. Paganini, on the other hand, benefitted from a congenital defect, an abnormal laxity of the fingerjoints which enabled, even tempted him, to play and compose virtuoso pieces for the violin.

The experience of disease has provided some authors, like Molière and Proust, with medical metaphors and has given others material for descriptions of disease, as we see in Charlotte Brontë, Chekhov, Goya and Marain Marais.

Disease may even act as an inducement. The degrading effect of physical deformities caused Byron and Toulouse-Lautrec to compensate through artistic work. The definite knowledge that the remaining working hours are limited has often given rise to a last blaze of intense activity as we have seen in Beardsley and Klee. Many, with Heine, Karen Blixen and Graham Greene have ascribed a therapeutic effect to creativity, a means of enduring the suffering of life. In *The Birth of Tragedy* Nietzsche says that it is only Art that has the power of diverting our feelings of disgust for a dreadful and meaningless existence into conceptions that one can live with.

Having asserted that he did not know a single day entirely free from pain since a childhood disease had left him forever a bundle of tics and tremors, Samuel Johnson concluded that "the only end of writing is to enable readers better to enjoy life or better to endure it". The Doctor himself, victim of severe periodic depression, was helped by his writing, "Employment, Sir, and hardships, prevent melancholy".

Finally, the most important and impressive influence of disease on artistic work is when it makes the whole character more serene, the keynote more profound. This, I think, has added to the lasting value of the fiction of Charlotte Brontë, the poetry of Keats, the late paintings of Cézanne and Rothko and the music of Chopin and Mahler.

✳ ✳ ✳

Realizing that some of the greatest art has been born of suffering, one is led to conclude that illness sometimes enriches the artist, his fellow men and posterity: "The suffering inspires the poet, gives greatness, sincerity and earnestness to his vision, stimulates his psychological imagination and gives pithy realism to his expressions of wrath and passion."[8]

One reaction is consistently present in the majority of artists, whatever their illness, namely a remarkable stoicism, even heroism, when confronted with this sort of ill fate. The urge and endeavour to achieve an original creation, to immortalize a personal conception, may overcome even extreme morbidity. In great artists, the passion to create generates a willpower strong enough to defeat the worst disease.

This tale of woe shall end in a lighter key with divine music celebrating a happy cure, as described on page 91.

In the beginning of the eighteenth century, Marin Marais composed a piece for viola da gamba describing the steps of an operation for stone in the bladder and the feelings of the patient. They are inscribed in the score, e.g. "The view of the operating table—trembling at the sight of it—serious thoughts—the incision—here the stone is delivered—here one nearly loses one's breath—blood is flowing—here one is put back to bed."

The relief is evident—after the ordeal of having brought forth his bladder stone, the composer expresses his feelings in no less than three gay dances, entitled Les Relevailles, "churching of a woman after childbirth!"—the happiest, indeed, of all human pain.

Illustrations

Frontispiece. A. Renoir, Self-portrait. Drawing, 1914 and Women in a landscape. Oil, 1919.

1. P. Mondrian, Composition with red. Oil, 1936. Priv. coll. © SPADEM, Paris 1982.

2. F. Kahlo, The broken column, 1944. Collection Dolores Olmedo.

3. F. Kahlo, What the water gave me. Oil, 1939, Detail © 1986 Sotheby's Inc.

4. A. Strindberg, Sea-marker in storm. Oil, 1892. Nationalmuseum, Stockholm.

5. G. Mahler, 5th Symphony, 1st movement, Facsimile, Courtesy Pierpont Morgan Library, New York.

6. H. Matisse, Figure décorative sur fond ornemental. Oil, 1927. Musée d'art Moderne, Paris.

7. H. Matisse, Nu bleu accroupi. Gouache découpée, 1952.

8. M. Utrillo, Moulin de la Galette. Oil, 1922. © SPADEM, Paris 1982.

9. M. Utrillo, Moulin de la Galette. Oil, 1953. Detail. © SPADEM, Paris 1982.

10. G. B. Piranesi, Carceri d'Invenzione. Engraving VII, 2nd ed., 1760.

11. M. C. Escher, Hol en bol. Lithograph, 1955. © SPADEM, Paris 1982.

12. J. Cocteau, Désintoxication. Drawing, 1929 (in Opium, Journal d'une désintoxication). © SPADEM, Paris 1982.

13. C. Baudelaire, Self-portrait. Drawing during hashish-intoxication.

14. H. Michaux, Mescaline drawing. Priv. coll.

15. C. F. Hill, Schizophrenic drawing. Malmö Museum.

16. F. Goya, El sueño de la razón produce monstruos. Engraving.

17. H. Linnqvist, Hospital ward. Oil, 1918. Priv. coll.
18. J. G. Sandberg, Samuel Ödman in bed. Oil,
    K. Vetenskapsakademien.
19. a, b, c. Anonymous. Schizophrene drawings. Spec-
    trum, Pfizer 4:177.
20. C. Méryon, La morgue. Engraving.
21. C. Méryon, Ministère de la Marine. Engraving.
22. E. Josephson, A summer's day in the pinewood. Oil,
    1885. Priv. coll.
22b. Michelangelo, ascribed to, Madonna and child with
    the infant baptist and angels (The Manchester
    Madonna – –) Detail. Panel. Reproduced by Cour-
    tesy of the Trustees, The National Gallery, London.
23. E. Josephson, The stage director. Oil, 1893. National-
    museum, Stockholm.
24. E. Munch, The shriek. Woodcut.
25. V. van Gogh, Portrait à l'oreille coupée. Oil, 1889.
    Coll. Leigh Block.
26. V. van Gogh, Wheatfield with Crows. Oil, 1890.
    Rijksmuseum Vincent van Gogh, Amsterdam.
27. Santeul, Le bossu. Facsimile 17th century.
28. H. de Toulouse-Lautrec, Self-portraits. Drawings.
    Edita, Lausanne.
29. D. Maclise, Paganini performing. Drawing, 1831.
    Courtesy, Bettmann arch. N.Y.C.
30. E. Delacroix, Jacob fighting with the angel. Oil.
    St. Sulpice, Paris.
31. P. Cézanne, Les grosses pommes. Oil, 1890. Priv. coll.
32. P. Cézanne, Pyramide de cranes. Oil, 1900.
33. P. Picasso, L'artiste et son modèle. Engraving, 1927.
    © SPADEM, Paris 1982.
34. P. Picasso, L'artiste et son modèle. Engraving, 1968.
    © SPADEM, Paris 1982.
35. A. Renoir, Self-portrait. Drawing.
36. P. Klee, Detaillierte Passion: Ein Gestalter. Drawing,
    1940. © 1982 by Cosmopress, Genève.

37a. R. Dufy, Flowers and handwriting while ill with rheumatism. Watercolour.

37b. R. Dufy, Flowers and handwriting when improved. Watercolour. Reprinted by permission of The New England Journal of Medicine.

38. El Greco, Burial of the Conde de Orgaz. Oil, 1586. Santo Tomé, Toledo.

39. E. Dickinson, Portrait. Daguerreotype. Amherst College. Reproduced by permission of the Trustees of Amherst College.
A. Dürer, Self-portrait. Drawing, 1491. Erlangen, Universitätsbibliothek.

40 F. Goya, Allegory on the adoption of the constitution. Oil, 1812. Nationalmuseum, Stockholm.

41. F. Goya, Saturn. Oil, 1820–23. Museo del Prado, Madrid.

42. J. P. Lyser, Beethoven. Drawing, 1823.

43. A. Böcklin, Toothache. Stone-relief, 1870. Kunsthalle, Basel.

44. F. Picabia, Paroxysme de la douleur. Oil, 1915. Coll. Simone Collinet. © SPADEM, Paris 1982. © A.D.A.G.P., Paris and Cosmopress, Genève.

45. H. Matisse, L'angoisse s'amasse. Linoleum-cut, 1940.

46. A. Watteau, The Medical Faculty. Engraving.

47. Anonymous. Operation for stone in the bladder. Engraving.

48. F. Goya, Donkey as doctor. Engraving.

49. F. Goya, Self-portrait with Dr Arrieta. Oil, 1820. Minneapolis Institute of Arts.

50. A. Watteau, La leçon d'amour. Oil, c. 1716–1717. Nationalmuseum, Stockholm.

51. Ch. Bronté, Portrait of Anne Bronté. Drawing. The Bronté Society.

52. H. Löwenhjelm, Death approaching. Wood-cut, 1919.

53. A. Beardsley, Pierrot dying. Drawing, 1897.

54. A. Beardsley, The artist tied to Priapus. Drawing.

55. A. Beardsley, Lysistrate. Drawing, 1896.

56. I. Arosenius, St. George and the dragon. Water-colour, 1903. Priv. coll.

57. I. Arosenius, Self-portrait on Pegasus. Watercolour.

58. I. Arosenius, Boy returning the golden goose. Water-colour, 1908. Priv. coll.

59. I. Arosenius, Macabre Company. Watercolour, 1908. Priv. coll.

60. P. Klee, Sängerhalle. India ink and watercolour, 1930. Priv. coll. © 1982 by Cosmopress, Genève.

61a. P. Klee, Durchhalten! Drawing, 1940. Paul Klee-Stiftung, Bern. © 1982 by Cosmopress, Genève.

61b. P. Klee, Photo.

62. P. Klee, Kranker im Boot. Drawing, 1940. Paul Klee-Stiftung, Bern. © 1982 by Cosmopress, Genève.

63. Hj. Gullberg, Poem with corrections. Facsimile. Lund University.

64. J. Gris, Nature morte au géranium. Oil, 1915. Priv. coll.

65. J. Gris, Nature morte avec pipe. Oil, 1926. Priv. coll.

Finale. M. Marais, Le Tableau de l'Opération de la Taille, and Les Relevailles. Facsimile. Pieces de Violes, Livre V, 1712. Bibliothèque Municipale, Lyon.

Tailpiece. A Monet, Le Bassin aux Nymphéas. Oil, 1900. The Art Institute of Chicago.
Le Pont Japonais à Giverny. Oil, c. 1923. The Minnea-polis Institute of Arts. © SPADEM, Paris 1984.
Le Pont Japonais. Oil, c. 1923?
Musée Marmottan, Paris. © SPADEM, Paris 1986.

Bibliography

1. Anonymous, *Psyko-ikonografi.* Spectrum-Pfizer 4 (1960), p. 177
2. Aragon, *Henri Matisse, Roman.* Paris 1971
3. Arnavon, Jacques, *Le Malade imaginaire de Molière.* Genève 1970
4. Bader and Navratil, *Zwischen Wahn und Wirkligkeit:* Kunst, Psychose, Kreativität. Lucerne 1976
5. Barzun, Jacques, Clio and the Doctors. Chicago 1974
6. Berefelt, Gunnar, *Notiser om psykopatologiskt bild-skapande.* Forskning och praktik 7 (1972), p. 73
7. Berlioz, Hector, *The Memoirs of Hector Berlioz.* New York 1969
8. Böök, Fredrik, *Esaias Tegnér.* Stockholm 1946
9. Bordonove, G., *Molière génial et familier.* Paris 1967
10. Bjurström, Per, *Arosenius.* Nationalmusei utst.kat. 410, 1978, p. 6
11. Björck, Staffan, *Sångaren och plågan.* Birger Sjöbergs-sällskapet 1966, p. 34
12. Butor, Michel, *Le Carré et son habitant.* Nouvelle revue Française 1961
13. Carstairs, G. M., *Art and psychotic illness.* Abbottempo
14. Cawthorne, F., *The influence of deafness on the creative instinct.* The Laryngoscope 70 (1969), p. 1110
15. Christy N. P. et al., *Gustav Mahler and his illnesses.* Trans. Am. Clin. and Climatol. Ass. 82 (1970), p. 200
16. Clark, Kenneth, *Civilization.* London 1969
17. Conrad, Joseph, *Letter to John Galsworthy,* 1908

18. Copleston, F., *Friedrich Nietzsche, philosopher of culture.* New York 1975

19. De Quincey, Thomas, *Confessions of an English Opium-Eater.* London 1821

20. Dickinson, Emily, *The complete poems of Emily Dickinson.* London 1979

21. Dinaux, A., *Watteau.* Paris 1834

22. l'Echevin, Patrick, *Musique et médecine.* Diss. Lille 1980

23. Edel, Leon, *Writing Lives,* New York 1984

24. Focillon, Henri, *Piranesi.* Paris 1928

25. Franken, F. H., *Krankheit und Tod grosser Komponisten.* Baden-Baden 1979

26. Glaesemer, J., *Paul Klee, Handzeichnungen* III. Bern 1979

27. Heller, K., *Michel de Montaignes Einfluss auf die Aerztestücke Molières.* Diss. Jena 1908

28. Herrera, H., *Frida.* Harper & Row. New York 1983

29. Hodge, G. P., *El Greco: on ending the myth of distorted vision.* Abbottempo in review. Chicago 1970, p. 88

30. Homburger F., and Bonner, D. D., *The treatment of Raoul Dufy's Arthritis.* New England Journ. of Med. 301 (1979), p. 669

31. Kant, Immanuel, *Von der Macht des Gemüths durch den blossen Vorsatz seiner krankhaften Gefühle Meister zu sein.* Hufeland

32. Kern, Ernst, *Zur Kulturgeschichte des Schmerzerlebnisses.* Hefte z. Unfallheilkunde 138 (1979), p. 9

33. Keller, Karl, *The only Kangaroo among the Beauty. Emily Dickinson and America.* Baltimore 1979

34. Kerner, Dieter, *Krankheiten grosser Musiker.* Stuttgart 1963

35. Kierkegaard, Søren, *Enten − eller.* København 1843

36. Kretschmer, Ernst, *Geniale Menschen.* Berlin 1929

37. Laing, Joyce H., *Tuberculous paintings.* Ciba Symposium 12 (1964), p. 135

38. Low, Marie DuMont, *Self in triplicate: the doctor in the nineteenth-century British novel.* University of Washington, 1973

39. Lundström, L.-J., *De artificiella paradisen.* Hässle 2 (1964), p. 5

40. ibid., *Charles Méryon, peintre-graveur schizophrène.* Acta Psychiatr. Scand. 40 (1964), p. 159

41. Mahler, Alma, *Gustav Mahler: Memoirs and Letters.* New York 1946

42. Matisse, Henri, *Propos recueillis par Régine Pernoud.* Le Courrier de l'UNESCO 1953, p. 6

43. Mondrian, Piet, *Plastic and pure plastic art.* London 1937

44. Morgenstern, Christian, *Gallow's Songs.* Translated by W. D. Snodgrass and Lore Segal. Univ. of Michigan Press, Ann Arbor 1967

45. Niederland, William G., *Psychoanalytic approaches to artistic creativity.* New York Acad. of Med. 1975

46. Nordenfalk, Carl, *The Stockholm Watteaus.* Nationalmuseum Bulletin 3 (1979), p, 105

47. Nordström, Folke, *Goya, Saturn and Melancholy.* Stockholm 1962

48. Ober, William B., *Boswell's clap and other essays.* Carbondale, Ill., 1979

49. O'Connor, Flannery, *The habit of being.* New York 1979

50. Pearson, Hesketh, *Walter Scott.* London 1954

51. Pickering, George W., *Creative malady.* London 1974

52. Ravin, James et al., *Mark Rothko's Paintings... Suicide Notes?* Ohio St. Med. J. 74 (1978) p. 78 ibid., *Monet's cataracts.* JAMA 253 (1985)

53. Sayre, Eleanor A., *Goya. A moment in time.* Nationalmuseum Bulletin 3 (1979), p. 28

54. Schopenhauer, Arthur, *Parerga und Paralipomena. 2.* Leipzig 1888

55. Shaw, George B., *Prefaces.* London 1934

56. Sontag, Susan, *Illness as metaphor.* New York 1978

57. Steegmuller, Francis, *The letters of Gustave Flaubert 1830–1857.* Cambridge, Mass. 1979

58. Stevenson, Robert L., *Ordered south.* London 1874

59. Tegnér, Esaias, *Tegnérs brev.* Utg. av Nils Palmborg, Malmö 1954 (Letter 6 Dec. 1818)

60. Topelius, Zachris, *Finnish Poet.*

61. Trevor Roper, P. D., *The World through Blunted Sight.* New York, 1970

62. Trilling, Lionel, *Introduction.* The selected letters of John Keats. New York 1951

63. Updike, John, *The City.* The New Yorker, 1982

64. ibid., *At war with my skin.* The New Yorker, 1985

65. Walser, Martin, *The World of Franz Kafka.* Ed. by J. P. Stern, New York 1980

66. Wand, Martin, and Sewall, Richard B., *"Eyes be blind, heart be still":* A new perspective on Emily Dickinson's eye problem. The New England Quarterly 52 (1979), p. 40

67. Weigand, Hermann, *The magic mountain. A study of Thomas Mann's novel.* Chapel Hill 1964

68. Weinberg, Steven, *The first three minutes.* London & New York 1977

69. Weintraub, Stanley, *Aubrey Beardsley, Imp of the Perverse.* Penn State Univ. Press 1976

70. ibid., *Medicine and the Biographers Art.* New York, 1980

71. Williams, Roger L., *The Horror of Life.* London 1980

72. Wilson, Edmund, *Philoctetes: the wound and the bow.* Cambridge, Mass. 1929

73. Wordsworth, W, Poems

74. Yourcenar, Marguerite, *Le cerveau noir de Piranèse.* Rome 1962

Index

Postscript

This fourth edition of *Creativity and Disease* the author regards, for the time being, as the definitive one. Some of the numerous additions and changes are due to continued flux in the discussion of diagnoses that must remain uncertain. The source of Beethoven's deafness, which seemed for a while ascertained, is again unknown, and there are new hypotheses about the cause of the rheumatism of Renoir and Dufy. The idea, discussed in previous editions, that le Douanier Rousseau painted portraits without ears because he lacked one himself I found was apocryphal.

Sections have been added on Milton, Chopin, Immanuel Kant and Rainer Maria Rilke. In the chapter on congenital malformations the Hunchback Song and a Madonna, ascribed to Michelangelo, have been included.

As the origin of this work dates back a quarter of a century I have naturally had much helpful advice over the years. Special thanks are due to Professor Ingmar Bengtsson of Uppsala University, Professor Staffan Björck of Lund University, Doctor Kaj Johansen of the University of Washington and Doctor Susanna Knott of San Diego. Mr Patrick Hort of Stockholm gave outstanding linguistic advice. Excellent secretarial help has been given by Mrs Winifred Boscacci and Mrs Antoinette Lucas of Lausanne and by Mrs Kerstin Hedin, Ystad, Sweden.

A part of nature, seen through
one and the same temperament
but through different eyes.

*The Japanese bridge in Monet's
garden in Giverny seen through the
healthy eyes of the great impressionist "He is only an eye – but what an
eye", said Cézanne.*

*Twenty years later, it is seen
through his cataracts, which filtered
away all colours except red and
yellow, which instead increased in intensity. The master noticed himself
that the colours became "odiously
false".*

*Finally the motif is seen through
eyes from which the opaque lens had
been removed, resulting in a rebound
of the colour perception toward the
blue end of the spectrum "It is filthy
– I see nothing but blue", the master
complained.*
   *With the help of tinted glasses
Monet returned to his original colour
scheme near the end of his life.*

142

Tailpiece

Claude Monet was one of the greatest colourists of all times. One can imagine his worry and alarm when cataract impaired his eyesight. The influence on his painting is pathetically evident. Forms grew vague and blurred. The brush strokes became coarse, sometimes violent as from desperation. His sense of colour changed and his palette veered to red when the opaque lens filtered out most other colours; even the blue turned purple.

After a cataract operation his sight was much improved. But Monet was not at all happy when he saw the red-tinted paintings from later years: "I know more than ever that the eyesight of a painter can never be recovered. When a singer loses his voice, he retires." He corrected the colour of some of his paintings; others he destroyed. Now that the cataract had gone, he exaggerated the blue instead–he knew this himself only from the paint tubes he chose, as they had been specially labelled. The red vision thus turned into blue: "It's filthy. It's disgusting. I see nothing but blue."

Eventually, however, his colour sense improved, much with the help of tinted glasses, and in peace he could finally, despite objections that he might spoil the pictures, complete his classic work, the large decorative paintings with ethereal water-lilies floating on the surface, which reflects the sky and a celestial light.